Jean-Baptiste de Lully
and his Tragédies Lyriques

Studies in Musicology, No. 1

Other Titles in This Series

Jean-Baptiste de Lully and his Tragédies Lyriques

by
Joyce Newman

RESEARCH PRESS

Library of Congress Cataloging in Publication Data

Newman, Joyce Enith Watkins, 1930-
  Formal structure and recitative in the tragédies
lyriques of Jean-Baptiste de Lully.

  (Studies in musicology series ; no. 1)
  Bibliography: p.
  Includes index.
  1. Lully, Jean Baptiste, 1632-1687. Operas. I. Title.
II. Series.

ML410.L95N5   782.1'092'4   79-12289
ISBN 0-8357-1002-5
ISBN 0-8357-1003-3 pbk.

Dedicated to my
Mother and Father

CONTENTS

INTRODUCTION

This study is an examination of the nature and uses of recitative in the *tragédies lyriques* of J.-B. de Lully. The dissertation will focus upon the following aspects of the works in question: literary elements, dramatic elements, and the music with especial reference to the interrelationship of these elements as determinants of form and technique. Although biographical and other extramusical factors will be examined and interpreted, this is not a biobibliographical study and, as the title indicates, concerns recitative in the *tragédie lyrique*. The arias, spectacles, and dances of the operas have been excluded as well as the ballets, pastorales, comedies, instrumental works, songs, and other of Lully's works except as they have a direct bearing on recitative in the *tragédie lyrique*.

The justification for this project lies in the current state of research into the works of Lully which examination reveals to be wanting in several important ways. Much that is badly needed for research simply is not readily available. Much that is available is incomplete, misleading, and sometimes downright erroneous. The following are exemplary of the problems encountered.

First, there is no modern edition of ten of the thirteen *tragédies lyriques*. Only three were completed by Henry Prunières before his death in 1942. The remaining ten are to be found either in manuscript form or as early printings and there are few complete collections. According to Prunières those operas written after 1679 are relatively easy to edit since they were printed the same year they were first performed under Lully's supervision by the firm Christophe Ballard.

Second, there has been no systematic study of the music of the *tragédies lyriques*, nor of the works themselves as a special creation whose processes and attributes remain those of French opera throughout its history. Etienne Gros, in his biography of Philippe Quinault, has written of the *tragédie lyrique* as a literary form. Cuthbert Girdlestone has extended that study to encompass the years 1673-1750, but once again the *tragédie lyrique* has been studied as a literary genre. The form and the interrelation of elements have never been the object of a study, nor are the distinguishing characteristics of the *tragédie lyrique* covered in any scholarly work. There are studies in general histories, for the works are of an importance which can hardly be ignored. Most of these works appear to be based on the three works from the Prunières edition with comments gleaned from study of the nineteenth century Lajarte edition wherein entire scenes have been cut with often as many as thirty or forty pages being omitted. Significantly, these cuts are most often of scenes written almost entirely in recitative.

Third, studies of recitative in Lully's works have been concerned chiefly with declamation rather than with the nature of the recitative itself.[1] Recitative has not concerned scholars to the extent that have arias, songs, and ensembles. This lack of interest is, perhaps, understandable in the case of operas in which the main emphasis is placed on arias linked together by *parlando* recitative; but in those works in which the elements of drama and music are more nearly balanced, the recitative is of primary importance. Such was the case with the *tragédie lyrique*.

Approximately half of each *tragédie lyrique* consists of recitative. There are few arias; a number of strophic songs and orchestral music are used to help link scenes together. The great choral spectacular scenes make up about a fourth or a fifth of each work. Examination of recitative in the thirteen operas showed that Lully was quite systematic in his uses of musical and dramatic elements. He gave the *tragédie lyrique* a structure which is a unique synthesis of elements from French dramatic forms, *ballet de cour*, Italian opera and orchestral music. This structure faithfully reflected Lully's own formation as an artist. He was forty years old when he turned to the *tragédie lyrique*, and it will be shown that although there is a distinct polishing of the style of writing evident in the thirteen *tragédies lyriques*, the basic creative process is the same in all of them.

Recitative in the French language was the only new element in the *tragédie lyrique*, and recitative is the framework Lully used to integrate the whole structure of the dramatic, vocal, instrumental, and spectacular elements taken from other theatrical forms. It is significant that those works of Lully which are heard today are isolated excerpts, vocal solos and ensembles, dances from spectacular scenes of the operas, and the play within the play from *Isis*. The recitative is inextricably interwoven with the drama and is used not merely as an introduction to aria, arioso and songs. For this reason, it is incomprehensible when extracted from its setting in the drama.

The ensuing pages will show how the dramatic works themselves evolved, how Lully's life and experience within musical and court circles tended to determine the form given to the *tragédie lyrique*, the manner in which the social and political trends of seventeenth century France influenced the operas, and, lastly, it will be demonstrated how recitative was used in order to create the internal structure of scenes in the *tragédie lyrique*.

NOTES

[1]Hugo Ritscher, "Die musikalische Deklamation in Lullys Opernrezitativen" (unpublished Ph.D. dissertation, University of Berlin, 1925).

CHAPTER I

THE *TRAGEDIE LYRIQUE*

Differentiation from Contemporary Dramatic Forms

The *tragédie lyrique* is one of several dramatic forms which evolved in seventeenth century France containing music, ballet, spectacle, machines, and instrumental music. Each of these forms has a particular name which attempts to describe the work exactly: *ballet de cour, ballet héroïque, comédie-ballet, tragi-comédie, tragi-comédie-pastorale, pastorale, pastorale héroïque*, and others. The terms are not interchangeable, and to use the generic term "opera" merely confuses the issue. This is not the place to define each of these terms, but some will be touched upon in order to give a clear definition of *tragédie lyrique*.

The *tragédie lyrique* is a tragedy completely set to music, and most of the characteristics which differentiate it from other forms are dramatic rather than musical. The plot is based on an incident in the life of a character of heroic proportions who passes from one state of being to another. If there are incidents and subplots, they are related to the main plot. The formal structure consists of a prologue and five acts, each of which is divided into several scenes. Each act is built around a single incident which is so constructed as to introduce some form of spectacle, either a ballet involving a large number of singers and dancers or the appearance of a miraculous machine. Linkage of scenes is observed throughout. Most often, linkage is through *présence*, and changes of scene even take place between the syllables of a word.

Unity of action is observed in the *tragédie lyrique*, but in some instances the various incidents which make up the acts are very closely woven into the main action, while in others the incidents are only loosely related to the main action. For example, in *Persée*, if the uniting of Persée and Andromède is considered to be the action, then the killing of Méduse, the conquering of the sea-monster, and the defeat of Phinée's army by Persée must be seen as the means of accomplishing the proper ending of the action rather than as three separate actions. Other *tragédies lyriques*, such as *Atys*, do not require such interpretation but instead are constructed from incidents which lead more directly to the denouement. Unity of place is not observed nor is any attempt made to observe it since the spectacular scene changes and variety of settings made this unity unobtainable. Unity of time is disregarded, and no mention of the passage of time would indicate whether or not this unity was being observed. The number of events taking place in each play, however, would occupy more than a full day. Meanwhile, any given scene conforms to the strict interpretation of unity of time (with the exception of battles and festivals), in that the incident takes the same amount of time to perform on the stage that it would take in reality.

The chorus and ballet play important roles in the *tragédie lyrique* for the chorus has been restored to the place of prominence it held in Greek and Roman tragedy as a commentator on the action and as an action in its own right. There are no requirements as to the number of characters, only the type. There are some comic characters and stock roles in the earlier *tragédies lyriques* written by Lully and Quinault.[1] Very often, identification of characters depends on prior knowledge of the story on which the *tragédie lyrique* is based.[2] The rules of propriety are strictly observed, characters behave according to their rank and state in life, and language is subdued. The amusingly free dialogue and songs of the earlier *tragédies lyriques* are not present in the later ones though they never could have been called lewd in any sense. The poetry is more varied than that of the tragedies of the classical stage where the Alexandrian couplet is the rule. In the *tragédie lyrique*, the couplet is combined with songs in lines of eight syllables and dialogue seems like free verse for the length of the line is often quite irregular.

The main conditions are that the piece first be tragic and then that it be sung throughout. The most important factor of all, however, is the character of the protagonist for it is he, or she, who defines the nature of a play. If this seems an artificial division, it should be remembered that Aristotle defined tragedy, comedy, and satyric drama according to the station in life and character of the protagonist as well as by the nature of the action and that the same definition was maintained by Seneca. The only change made by the Renaissance authors was to change satyrs into shepherds and, thus, the satyric drama into the pastorale. It is significant that Pierre Corneille, in the *Discours* which accompanied the first publication of his works, stated that a comedy might also have a king in it, but in that case it should be entitled *comédie héroique*.[3]

Therefore, the *tragédie lyrique* must contain elements which are barred from the *tragédie* proper (that is, ballet, chorus, songs, machines and spectacles, and instrumental interludes). The main differences between *tragédie lyrique* and the pastorale, *ballet-comédie*, and other such forms are those very things which characterize spoken drama, and it was by the criteria of spoken drama that the *tragédie lyrique* was judged by Boileau (and others!) who criticized it not because it contained poor music but because it did not conform to his concept of *tragédie*. To understand a work of art, it is necessary to accept the conventions which underlie its creation. No study of the *tragédie lyrique* can be complete unless those literary and dramatic elements are examined which more than the music, serve to distinguish it from all other forms.

Greek and Roman Influence

The *tragédie lyrique* was a combination of the various types of drama being played in seventeenth-century France. These forms of dramatic literature were the products of a very long tradition going back to Greek drama, itself an outgrowth of religious observances of which music was an integral part. Aristotle described the theater of the Greeks in his *Poetics* and, at the same time, he set a pattern for literary criticism which was followed by various authors in subsequent centuries who referred to this work. The Greek plays were performed by the Romans who made their own additions and over a period of some five hundred years, modified the practices of their predecessors. Greek and Roman theater never completely died out but was, on the contrary, performed in schools and courts throughout the Middle Ages while wandering street players maintained the traditions of a more humble sort of theater with even more ancient origins. In the Renaissance a renewed interest arose not only in the plays of the Ancients themselves but also in the *Poetics* of Aristotle which was again available in the original, though many errors in interpretation of Aristotle's work resulted from the great number of French translations of Latin translations. Discussion in the various academies and universities centered around the exact nature of classical drama and, eventually, there was much imitation of the Ancients.

The three basic types of classical drama are tragedy, comedy, and satyric drama, or pastorale. They are defined and differentiated by the state in life of the main character and by the nature of the action, and it should be understood that the ending makes little difference in classification. The Roman architect, Vitruvius, described stage-settings of these three kinds in his *De Architectura* as: tragic, comic, and satyric.[4] Leon Battista Alberti, in his *De Re Aedificatoria* (1485), not only described the settings but also characterized the dramas for which they are designed.

> Since three kinds of poets affect the theater, the tragic who recite the miseries of tyrants, the comic who set forth the cares and troubles of family-men *(patres-familias)*, the satyric who sing the amenities of the countryside and the cares of the shepherds *(ruris amoenitates pastorumque curas)* their appropriate settings are court, or house or woodland *(seu attrium seu casa, seu etiam sylva).*[5]

These remained the basic three genres of theater in the seventeenth century, and if the names given to various forms of theater are related to the nature of the protagonist and the action, it will be found that the terms are largely self-explanatory. A tragedy, then, is about a character or characters of noble proportions, comedy is about everyday men and women and the various emotions and events which are common in all human life, while the satyric drama or the pastorale is concerned with rural life.

The principles of poetic and dramatic structure set forth by Aristotle became the basis of all written drama in Lully's day. Aristotle sets no rules, no unities, no fixed proposals, but rather he made observations, giving examples of both good and bad practices and suggesting means of improving poetical works. He spoke of poetry as imitation and of the nature and forms which imitation takes and described the origins of poetry--tragedy, comedy, and epic. Of time, he says,

> They--epic and tragedy--also differ in length, for tragedy tries to confine itself, as much as possible, within one revolution of the sun or a little more, whereas the time of an epic is unlimited. This, however, was at first true also of tragedy.[6]

He defined the six elements of tragedy: plot, character, thought, diction, music, and spectacle. The key statement concerning unity of action occurs in the section on plot.

> As in other kinds of imitative art each imitation must have one object, so with plot: since it is the imitation of an action, this must be one action and the whole of it; the various incidents must be so constructed that, if any part is displaced or deleted, the whole plot is disturbed and dislocated.[7]

In describing the character of the protagonist, he says,

> A man who is neither outstanding in virtue and righteousness, nor is it through wickedness and vice that he falls into misfortune, but through some flaw. He should also be famous and prosperous, like Oedipus, Thyestes, and the noted men of noble families.[8]

He spoke of consistency and appropriateness of speech, action, and behaviour of the character. He also stated that it is possible, though unlikely, for a woman or even a slave to have noble stature.[9]

Aristotle named the divisions of tragedy prologue, episode and exodus.

> The *prologos* is that whole section which precedes the entrance of the chorus; the *episodion* is a whole section between complete choral odes; the *exodos* is that whole section of a tragedy which is not followed by a choral ode. In the choral part, the entrance song

(*parodos*) is the first complete statement of the chorus, a *stasimon* is
a song of the chorus without anapeste or trochee; a *kommos* is a
dirge in which actors and chorus join.[10]

The manner of deployment of materials is described showing
how recognition and the unfolding of the story should proceed, the use
of natural as compared with supernatural means, and how
characterization is best used to produce a tragedy which moves the
audience. He speaks of the method of writing of the poet, the need to
visualize the play, and to work from an outline. The poet must also be
emotionally involved with his characters. There are four types of
tragedy:

> The complex tragedy in which reversal and recognition are the whole
> drama; the tragedy of suffering, like the plays of Ajax or Ixion; the
> tragedy of character, like the Pythian women and Peleus; and fourth,
> the spectacular tragedy, like the Daughter of Phorcys, the
> Prometheus, and all the plays that are located in the Underworld.[11]

He spoke of the role of the chorus as a character in the play.
He considered diction, modes of expression, the parts of a speech,
compound words, metaphors, and, finally, he concluded his work with a
section on criticism.

From this very brief sketch of Aristotle's *Poetics* it can be seen
that those very elements which tend to characterize the *tragédie lyrique*
were set forth first in this work. There are many modifications by
subsequent authors and critics but the following factors remained. The
nature of theater is defined and the six elements are named: plot,
character, thought, diction, music, and spectacle. Plot is restricted to a
single action, or rather only incidents which can be related to a single
action. Extensive cuts in Lully's *tragédies lyriques* result in the whole
plot's being "disturbed and dislocated"--just as Aristotle warned would
be the case in a play properly constructed. The character of the
protagonist is set, as is the necessity of a change of fortune brought about
through the character of the protagonist. Aristotle said that both natural
and supernatural means may be used in bringing about the denouement
(though he preferred natural means, while in the *tragédie lyrique* the
means preferred are supernatural). The catastrophe must be a "fall"
according to Aristotle, whereas later the change of fortune is all that is
necessary. The question of propriety and the appropriateness of action
and speech is raised although it was even more violently debated in the
seventeenth century on the same principles.

The division of a drama into sections is based on the presence of
choral scenes. Recognition, unraveling, the supernatural, and the use of
characterization to produce good drama are all treated by Aristotle and

his suggestions are to be found materialized in *tragédie lyrique*. The four types of tragedy named by Aristotle do provide the basis for description of all thirteen *tragédies lyriques*, for *Atys* is a tragedy of suffering, *Thésée* is a tragedy of recognition and reversal, *Phaéton* is a tragedy of character, and *Proserpine* is a tragedy of spectacle. However, it must be understood that these are merely examples which occur through imitation. Above all, spectacle is to be found in all of the *tragédies lyriques*. Interestingly, the chorus was barred from tragedy in the late sixteenth century in France, it was present in the early Florentine operas because of the conscious imitation of the Ancients, barred once more from opera in seventeenth century Venice only to reappear in the *tragédie lyrique.*

In short, a pattern was set by Aristotle to which both poets and critics have returned ever since until quite recently. It should also be stressed that few plays are written to conform with rules and formulae, and that critics and theorists tend to describe a style which is already out of date at the time they write. Nevertheless, such works are invaluable for they tell about those things which are not written down in the texts of plays and also give the names of works and authors which otherwise would be completely lost.

Horace, a Roman satyric poet and moralist who died in the year A.D. 8, also wrote an "Art of Poetry." This work, itself in poetry, is not as extensive as that of Aristotle, but certain phrases within it show that the Roman authors had made changes which became characteristics of later theater and of French opera as well.

> Five acts are the just measure of a play. . . .[12]
>
> And in one scene no more than three should speak. . . .[13]
>
> Some things are acted, others only told;
> But what we hear moves less than what we see.[14]
>
> Yet there are things improper for a scene,
> Which men of judgment only will relate.[15]
>
> A chorus should supply what action wants,
> And hath a generous and manly part;[16]
>
> But nothing must be sung between the acts
> But what some way conduces to the plot.[17]
>
> Gods, heroes, conquerors, Olympic crowns,
> Love's pleasing cares, and the free joys of wine,
> Are proper subjects for the lyric song.[18]

Here, then, is the prescription of five acts as the proper structure for a play. There is a suggestion that scenes are to be defined by the actors present, a fact better shown in the Roman dramas themselves, for the structure of the stage demanded that scene changes be shown by verbal means such as, "Oh, look, here comes. . ." the problem being how to make a whole action take place on a single stage[19] and how to account for the passage of time. The third quotation contains an observation concerning the practice of setting action in a lengthy monologue,[20] a fact of considerable importance to their setting by Lully as well as to how he staged them. The Quinault monologues are so organized as to portray a significant change in the action or direction of the plot rather than to serve as mere explanation. The next quotation is an attempt to keep the brutal and licentious from being enacted in full view, a practice which had become common on the Roman stage.[21] The role of the chorus is defined and its importance emphasized, for it was being relegated to a position of minor importance since the Roman actors loved their monologues and songs. Nothing sung between the acts--this is not a bid for unity of action but refers instead to the practice of having popular players from the streets improvise scenes before, after, and, it would seem, between the acts of a regular drama. Horace amplifies some of the points made by Aristotle while bringing out some of the practices which had become popular and common to the Roman stage. This is fortunate for all the Roman plays which have been preserved can be contained in two volumes though many more plays are known through commentaries written about them which contain their titles.

The plays of Seneca are those on which the Italians of the Renaissance modeled their own. This was due at least in part to their availability. These plays were not designed for performance at all, and according to some authors never were performed in ancient Rome,[22] but they did attract the interest of scholars and they were staged in the early universities. Scholastic performance and memorization of the entire texts gave the Senecan tragedy such a widespread public that when Aristotle's *Poetics* were studied, the critics and theorists of the Renaissance were obliged to make whatever modifications were necessary to make the Greek theories conform to the Roman models derived from them.[23]

The concept of virtue as a companion of self-restraint, dependent as it is on the exercise of freedom of will, was particularly attractive to the Renaissance mind. The same concept is portrayed repeatedly in the *tragédies lyriques*. Seneca was one of Rome's outstanding Stoic philosophers, and the didactic element is stressed in his plays. He was most influenced by Euripides, but even when his plays are most clearly modeled on those of Euripides he nevertheless transforms them to conform more nearly to the taste of his day. This technique also is to be found in French seventeenth-century theater as will be discussed in Chapter III. Seneca gives greater or lesser importance to one or another character, lengthens or shortens the action, and makes whatever alterations are necessary to present the stories in a different light. In general, he concentrates interest on the main characters and subordinates minor incidents. Since the Romans were not nearly as involved with the religious element which had played such a role in Greek drama, Seneca reinterpreted the stories in such a way as to portray the incidents on a human plane. Here it is the complex character of man and his manner of living which bring about misfortune, not fate or the gods. Seneca enjoyed theatrical effects and wrote many scenes in which the supernatural appears in ghost scenes and pseudo-religious invocations and divinations.[24]

The formal structure is that of five acts, or parts, each of which terminates with a choral passage. The chorus takes no part in the action, but it shows the author's feeling towards his characters and, therefore, indicates how the audience should react.[25] The prologue is the first act and is spoken by a supernatural character who makes many allusions to the coming play. Seneca, like the later writers of tragedy, took for granted that his audience had a great deal of previous knowledge of the story and, therefore, used references to shorten scenes and sequences.[26] This is quite different from the Greeks but entirely similar to the treatment given to mythological subjects in seventeenth-century France. His plots deal chiefly with love, hatred, and revenge, and he makes use of rhetorical devices (also characteristics of the French seventeenth century drama). Though the plays of Seneca exercised a direct influence on French tragedy, they also exercised an indirect influence through the Italian plays derived from them.

The Contribution of Italian Renaissance Drama

Italian Renaissance tragedy in imitation of Seneca was first written in Latin. Albertino Mussato wrote *Ecerinis* in about 1314 on a subject drawn from contemporary history, the death of the tyrant of Padua. Other Latin tragedies followed. Along with the adoption of the vernacular for poetry in the fifteenth century came attempts at drama in Italian. The first landmark in tragedy in the Italian tongue was the *Sophonisba* of Trissino, written in 1515 and published in 1524. It was presented in public for the first time in Vicenza in 1562, twelve years after the poet's death. Translated into French by Mellin de St. Gelais in 1553, it soon became one of the perenially popular subjects for drama.[27] The same subject was also treated by Alfieri, Montchrestien, Mairet, Corneille, Voltaire, Marston, Lee, Thompson, and in 1914 by Gabrielle d'Annunzio in the movie, *Cabiria*.

Trissino was consciously trying to imitate the ancient Greeks (especially Aristotle) and his chief rival, Giraldi Cinzio, imitated the Romans, particularly Seneca. Both men wrote critically of the theater and their feelings concerning it.[28] Cinzio's plays, however, were more effective with the Renaissance public and cther tragedies were written on the Senecan model. Both Trissino and Cinzio observed the unities of action and of time with the result that unity of place was often observed as well. The Renaissance authors added the possibility of a happy ending and used the term *tragicommedia* for such works. They frequently emphasized the emotional and blood-thirsty element of Roman tragedy and brought violence back to the stage with gruesome murders taking place in full view of the public or with the messenger announcing a murder or revenge while waving some member of the deceased in the front of the audience to illustrate his statements. The settings for the production of plays became lavish, and theaters were constructed to perform them.[29] Often a series of plays were produced in celebration of some royal or semiroyal festival.

The influence of Renaissance comedy on French opera, though far less potent than that of tragedy and pastorale, cannot be ignored. Italian comedy, based on the plays of Terence and Plautus, contained intermezzi consisting of ballet and mythological pageantry which utilized machines.[30] Like tragedy, comedy was produced at courts and in the universities, especially in Rome and Ferrara. The most popular vernacular works based on the Roman models were those of Ariosto who wrote five comedies, the *Mandragola* of Macchiavelli, and the five comedies of Pietro Aretino. One of the appeals of comedy was the magnificence of its presentation, and when Ariosto's *I Suppositi* was played at the Vatican in 1519, the scenery was painted by Rafael Sanzio. While the character of the protagonist is the most important part of tragedy, the plot, facetious situations, and witticisms are the most important element in comedy. The situations were drawn from real life, the humor is broad, and the ridiculousness of the lives of everyday people is emphasized. Thus, the braggart, the hypocrite, the flighty woman, the debauched old man, the predatory nature of women, the old man with the young wife, the philandering priest, and the naïveté of all as they progress through their self-deceptions is exposed for the amusement and instruction of the audience.

In addition to the written comedy there existed an improvised comic genre, the *commedia dell'arte*, played by travelling companies of actors who always portrayed the same characters.[31] Italian companies playing the *commedia* travelled all over Europe and established themselves as resident theaters in many large cities. So close to human nature are the characters of the *commedia dell'arte* that remnants of it exist today. One of the important features of these stock-companies was that the individual actors owned their own costumes. The sets belonged to the entire company, and the profits from public performances were divided by shares. It was self-supporting, and actors, while outside the pale of society, were nevertheless free agents who did not depend on feudal lords for their lives and rights. Certain of their leaders became famous, as for example, Scaramuccia. Eventually this form of organization became that of the theatrical troupes of Paris, the *Comédiens du Roi* at the Hôtel de Bourgogne, the Théâtre Marais, the troup of Molière at the Palais-Royal, and, finally, the same structure was modified slightly by Lully and made that of the opera, of which more later. Lully made use of stock characters derived from the *commedia dell'arte* in his first two *tragédies lyriques*, and it is surely no accident that he cast himself as Scaramouche in two of his *ballets de cour.*

Several characteristics peculiar to the pastorale also were adopted in French seventeenth-century opera. The pastorale was perfected by Tasso and Guarini, and it spread throughout Europe. The plays are cast in five acts with scene divisions. They contain lyric choruses, are written in blank verse, and are based on love-tangles.[32]

Pastorales were given in sumptuous settings, enlivened by music, ballet and spectacular interludes and presented out of doors. As a literary genre, they lack interest except in the hands of the very finest poets, but as entertainment for a sophisticated audience they surpassed both tragedy and comedy and were, at the end of the sixteenth century, the most popular form of theater.

From the pastorale to opera was not really a revolutionary step, for the form was actually a type of theater piece with spoken dialogue interspersed with a great number of songs. The discussions amongst the poets and authors as to what drama should be according to the writings of Aristotle led to the formation of opera in Florence. These men were, for the most part, less musicians than they were philosophers. The history of the development of monody and of the opera has received detailed presentation elsewhere and will not be treated here, but it is significant that the pastorale was the literary genre chosen for the complete setting to music.

There are significant differences in the subsequent history of Italian and French opera. In Italy, opera based on the pastorale was originally a part of court entertainment, and after a period of development lasting approximately thirty years it became a public entertainment with the construction of the opera houses in Venice. Opera in Italy became so popular that it eventually dominated the stage to such a degree that there was a distinct decline in dramatic literature which did not contain music. In France, though opera developed nearly seventy-five years after it was developed in Italy, its history is strikingly different. Though Lully and Quinault called it *tragédie lyrique* indicating that it was basically a tragedy, it would be more accurate to state that it was based sometimes on tragi-comedy, sometimes tragedy, and that it incorporated all of the devices of the machine play and *ballet de cour* as well--in short, all of the tested and popular theatrical practices of the mid-seventeenth century French theater.   It was first produced for a paying public and, therefore, had to please not only royalty and nobility but also the lesser public which occupied the *parterre* and the critics. Furthermore, over one thousand dramatic works with and without music had been produced in Paris during the first three-quarters of the seventeenth century, some of which were so well received that they were presented forty or fifty times in a single season.[33]   Opera in France did not supplant the theater as it did in Italy, as from the beginning it was more dependent on dramatic forms.

French Theater Before 1670

It is beyond the scope of this work to trace the history of the French theater in detail, but to understand the interaction of it with the imported Italian genres it is necessary to sketch its development briefly. Much has been made of the fact that Adam de la Halle's *Jeu de Robin et Marion* was the first pastorale and that it contained music.   It was the plays which grew out of the practice of trooping, however, that were the real source from which French theater developed.   From the liturgical drama grew the mysteries and the miracle plays. The stock devices used in these dramas were adapted for use in tragedy, comedy, and pastorale.

Saint-Beuve criticized the mysteries severely, comparing their successive scenes to an intermittent frieze without unifying principles.[34] The mysteries were performed with elaborate stage settings and machinery, sometimes with as many as five hundred actors, and acquired interpolations taken from everyday contemporary life. Biblical characters mixed with street people, damned souls played like clowns, the religious and the profane, tragic and comic, lovely and grotesque were indiscriminately mixed. The mysteries were extremely popular, and all business would come to a halt as entire towns turned out to attend the productions which lasted for different lengths of time varying from a few days to several weeks.

As in Italy, the history of the comic theater in France is difficult to trace, and the subdivision into *moralités, sotties, farces, monologues*, and *sermons joyeux* makes the question even more complex.   However, for the development of the *tragédie lyrique* it is important to note that there were independent short, comic plays, while in the mysteries, comic sequences were maintained side by side with the tragic, religious, and didactic.

Most important for the development of drama was the organization of dramatic societies of players with monopolies to produce one or another type of theater. Far from being the invention of Colbert, Perrin, or Lully, this type of patent had existed for hundreds of years. The *Basoche*, made up of clerks of the parliament or courts was chartered in 1303 under Philippe le Bel as a kingdom with officials and privileges. The *Confrèrie de la Passion* received a charter from Charles VI in 1402 permitting it to give plays taken from the Passion, Resurrection, and other portions of the Bible. The *Confrèrie* was established at the Hôtel de Bourgogne, and in 1548 they were granted a monopoly of the stage but were forbidden to act any mysteries. They did not immediately adopt the Renaissance humanist plays, but the Italian influence was beginning to be felt. At the turn of the century the actor-manager, Valleran Lecomte, appears to have been the person most instrumental in transforming the *Confrèrie de la Passion* into *les Comédiens du roi* who acted plays of all kinds.[35]

About 1634 another actor-manager, Montdory, established a rival troupe at the Théâtre du Marais. Montdory was a tragedian, and it was at the Marais that the works of Pierre Corneille were introduced. Montdory had with him a writer of plays, Alexandre Hardy, who did much in his hundreds of plays, to draw the drama into a more concise structure by cutting the lyric choruses and intensifying the action. In this way, the *tragédie* became in France the theatrical work which did not contain music.[36] Hardy is also thought of as the creator of the French *tragi-comédie.*

In 1629, Jean Mairet, influenced by the Count de Cramail and the Cardinal de la Valette, wrote a pastorale, *Silvanire,* and set forth his principles of organization in a preface in poetic form. He states that he has written his plays in accordance with the rules of the Italians who were themselves inspired by the Greeks and Romans particularly Tasso, Guarini, and Guidobaldi, each of whom wrote a single pastorale which made him more famous than many men who wrote more than two hundred poems.[37] The rules Mairet referred to were the famous unities of time, action, and place. Though this is the first actual statement of observance of the unities in France, the whole question of regularizing the drama was of great concern to authors and public. Imitation of *Aminta* and *Sophonisba* automatically led to the observance of the unities as portrayed by the Italians. However, the unities were not adopted instantly or accepted universally.

Pierre Corneille observes the unities partially in some of his plays but, like the majority of authors, he is far from making them a fixed rule. Interestingly, Jean Louis Guez de Balzac speaks in a letter of a lady who did not have the patience to watch a comedy not written within the twenty-four-hour rule.[38] In fact, the unities first were developed and applied in the pastorale, comedy, and tragi-comedy before the tragedy had become the crowning glory of the French stage, as well as being the dramatic genre in which the unities were most severely applied. Furthermore, it is only the later literary criticism, e.g., the controversy over *Le Cid*, which has led to the belief that tragedy was judged according to how well it adhered to the rules and the concept that the French are more concerned with the form than with the content of a dramatic work. In actual fact, dramatic forms in France developed from such a variety of theatrical practices, native, Italian and Spanish, that the real problem was to achieve coherence. This problem was not only a question of producing better works, but also of gathering public support because the dramatic companies existed solely by their capacity to draw an audience. Spectacular scenes, good music, fine costumes, and startling events were not enough to hold the interest of a cultivated public after the novelty of the first productions wore off.

The unities served an important purpose in that they caused the authors of dramatic works to make their plays more concise. Unity of action tended to eliminate the variety of plots and subplots, disconnected incidents, and made the drama into a cohesive whole, the excitement of which did not abate from beginning to end. Unity of time, always debatable (was a day twelve hours, twenty-four, or was it limited to the actual time of the play?), tends to follow unity of action automatically. Unity of place reduced the setting from the universal depiction of the mysteries to a concise and restricted area easily encompassed by the audience. This unity also tended to be observed automatically with the observance of unity of action. The result was far better drama for, in limiting the subject matter to be covered, the authors were forced to depict that material more fully while the distribution of incidents bearing on a single action throughout the five acts caused the tension to mount inexorably to the denouement.

At the beginning of the seventeenth century there remained a single dramatic problem to be solved: linkage, or liaisons between scenes. Even with the unity of action demanding that all events be connected with a single action, dramatic continuity was not assured, for it is quite possible to have two scenes which are connected with a single main theme and nevertheless be completely disconnected with each other.

Originally, a change of scene signified a change of place and gradually the meaning changed to become a change of character. The settings of the mystery in the *cour des miracles* make the term "scene-change" quite easily understood, for one scene would be set on one side of the court courtyard and another elsewhere, leading to charming stage directions and terms such as *les enfants du paradis doivent chanter*. However, the scenes in the mysteries were also highly disconnected both in place and in character, first religious, then vulgar and profane, and by turns also sentimental.

The adoption of the unities, especially those of action and place, had a profound effect on the structure of scenes. If the interpretation of place is strict, that is, confined within a single room, or, if outdoors, encompassed in the distance at which a man can easily recognize another man, then of necessity, the scene (in the sense of setting) did not change at all. Furthermore, unity of action had an equally narrowing effect on actual scene changes, for only with great difficulty could dramatists persuade themselves and the critics that a scene which took place in an exotic foreign country such as Cathay, was an integral portion of an action which was taken from Greek mythology. Meanwhile the disjointedness caused by the inclusion of spectacles and machine scenes was nevertheless adopted into drama of the early seventeenth century.

Lack of continuity between scenes was increased by the fact that according to the rules of dispersion of materials in the acts, the characters were to be presented in the first act, regardless of their place in the action.

Finally, in addition to the whole question of rules, there is yet another consideration; a poet is not at all necessarily a dramatist. D'Aubignac, in imitation of Aristotle, wrote a "Pratique du Théâtre" in which he says,

> But when our poets begun to write for the Stage, they hardly knew what an act or a scene was; they plac'd a Man upon the Stage, to recite there what they had composed for him, and they took him away again when the CAPRICIO of their Muse pleas'd, and then brought on one or more, which went off with as little reason; so that one might have transposed any of their SCENES, without any injury to the PLAY, every one of them making as it were an ACT by itself. We have seen upon our Stage a Captain, a Poet, and a Visionary Lover, all without having anything to do with one another; and what they said was more like so many Scholars Declamations, without any dependency on each other.[39]

Linkage of scenes, therefore, was a dramatic necessity. Authors around 1630 explain in prefaces to the printed versions of their plays that the scenes are linked.[40] Furthermore, this linkage takes place first in plays where unity of action is not observed, and, therefore, linkage can be considered as yet another manner of obtaining a more cohesive dramatic structure. When linkage of scenes is combined with unity of place no actual change of setting occurs. Change of scene, therefore, came to mean not change of setting but a change of character. Even more precisely, each scene is built around one or another of the principal characters of the drama rather than around a place or happening, though obviously the two things will often coincide. The essential element, however, is the change of character and the problem is establishing continuity. Sometimes scenes continue the action of the previous scene without any shift in time or action. Sometimes, on the contrary, an indefinite amount of time has elapsed between the end of one scene and the beginning of the next, and the action is also quite different in context and relation to the main theme. If unity of place is interpreted to mean that two different sections of a palace, or of a forest, or any other setting within certain limits can be used, then not only does an indefinite amount of time elapse between scenes, but also, in all likelihood, there was no connection between the two scenes whatsoever except that both are related to the main action. Such scene changes often took place before the delighted eyes of the audience just as children and adults thrill today to see the Christmas tree grow into an enchanted forest in the *Nutcracker* ballet.

D'Aubignac described linkage as follows:

> Now I have observed that there are four ways of uniting the scenes together; to wit, an Union of *presence*, another of *seeking*, a third of *noise* and a fourth of *time*.[41]

Union of presence can be achieved in three ways; by bringing on all the characters of an act at once and having them retire one by one, which D'Aubignac advises for the first act; secondly, to have them come on stage one by one and remain until the end of the act which he feels is suitable for the last act. The third way, capable of most variety, occurs when actors enter and leave the stage according to their business and interests.

Seeking, noise, and *time* are less used manners of linking scenes though they are effective for variety. *Seeking* occurs when an actor enters looking for another who has just left. *Noise* occurs when a sound is made on stage and an actor comes to see what caused it. Linkage of time is explained by D'Aubignac:

> . . .'tis when an Actor, who has nothing to do with those who go off the stage, comes on, but in such a nick of time, that he could not reasonably be suppos'd to do it sooner or later.[42]

The example which he gives shows that this linkage could just as well be called "reasonable hazard" for the actor just happens to come on stage at that moment for reasons of his own, independent of the scene and thus causing a new scene!

The linkage of scenes was adopted from the drama into the *tragédie lyrique.* Quinault is, in fact, extremely conscientious in his use of linkage probably because he makes heavy demands on the previous knowledge of plot so that incidents are telescoped into a word or a song without which the subsequent action is incomprehensible were it not for previous knowledge on the part of the audience. Most often, Quinault uses linkage of presence of the third sort described by D'Aubignac, that is, when actors come on and leave the stage according to their business and interests. He takes care to see that the stage is never empty, and in the printed editions of his *tragédies lyriques* scene changes often take place between the syllables of a word.

The principles of theater presented in D'Aubignac's *Pratique du théâtre* are those which came to typify French *tragédie*. The work was esteemed by Boileau, and Racine annotated it as he did parts of Aristotle's *Poetics*.[43] *Tragédie lyrique* was affected by it in its formation and was criticized according to it. The main principles of the *Pratique* follow.[44]

The subject should not be invented, but rather borrowed. Subjects should portray a great passion, an intrigue, or some great spectacle. They should be reduced to those elements which will not shock the opinions or feelings of the audience. Action must not lag, and something new should be presented in each act and, if possible, each scene. Unity of place means a single room, or if out of doors, a setting not large enough to prevent recognition of one person by another. Unity of time is interpreted to mean an interval of time identical with the performance but can be extended to the artificial day, that is, about twelve hours. Time and place must be indicated in the text itself. Incidents should be prepared, but the audience should not be able to guess what is coming. The prologue and chorus are to be discarded in *tragédie* as ancient practices not suited to modern taste. The five acts should contain almost equal amounts of material, but if there is a discrepancy, there should be more material in the later acts than in the earlier. There should be an incident or an emotion in each act--there may be more than one, but not many in order not to overexcite the audience. The stage should never be empty during an act. The same actor should not end one act and begin the next except in comedy. Each act should bring the end of the action, not merely the departure of the actors as in a scene. The catastrophe is the final change of fortune; it should be clear, well prepared, and end the intrigue. It can be happy or unhappy; in the former case the play can be called a tragi-comedy.

Three years after the appearance of this work, Corneille's three *Discours* on theater appeared in the 1660 edition of his plays.[45] Quite naturally, those works tend to justify the author's own practices excepting those instances wherein he had changed his mind since writing one or another of his plays. His importance as a dramatist was such that his *Discours* was placed side by side with d'Aubignac's *Pratique*. Unfortunately, Corneille, who did not at all apply the unities with rigidity, included some remarks to the effect that if d'Aubignac had written a few plays himself, he would have been more liberal in his interpretation of the rules. This was a double insult, for d'Aubignac had indeed written a few plays, but they had been unsuccessful and, furthermore, d'Aubignac felt that he had included several chapters in his work which contained preeminently practical advice to dramatists. D'Aubignac answered Corneille's remarks by expurgating all of the favorable comments he had made in his first edition of the *Pratique*; however, the second, anti-Corneillian edition was never published.

According to Corneille, the object of poetry is to please, and the rules are those of the art itself which are drawn from reason rather than from the practice of the Ancients. Morality, he says, should be portrayed both by the story itself and the modern use of maxims, and while the punishment of vice and the reward of virtue are not rules of art, they do help a play to succeed. He misinterprets *katharsis* to mean the moral force of example and doubts its usefulness. Kings and princes can appear also in comedy as well as tragedy, but in that case it should be called *comédie héroïque*. (From this we may conclude that the terms *ballet héroïque* and *pastorale héroïque* have similar meanings.) Love is not a sufficiently important passion for tragedy, though it should be introduced. Honor is the appropriate passion. The ending of a comedy must be happy, that of a tragedy can be happy or not as the author sees fit. Characters can be of any sort but their behavior must be suitable to their age, rank, birth, and station in life. He does not go so far as to say that older men cannot be in love. They can, but they use arguments different from those of young men to win the objects of their affections. Historical characters should not be altered. Diction should be clear, figures of speech appropriately used. Verse is better than prose but it should not be affected. Songs can be used in scenes with machines. Corneille wrote that he esteemed plays in which there is a conflict between passion and "nature" (i.e., family relationships such as the conflict portrayed in *Romeo and Juliet*), between love and honor. He thought that many of the inventions of authors were not as good as the true and real. His interpretation of the unities is much broader than d'Aubignac's. The unity of time is extended to about thirty hours, the place to two or three localities within a single city, but the ideal is as restricted as possible. Instead of being quite clear about this in the text of the play as d'Aubignac advised, Corneille prefers that these questions should remain vague. For liaisons, Corneille favors *liaison de présence*, like d'Aubignac. He does not mention linkage of time, he admits linkage of seeking and of noise, though he dislikes the latter. He includes another form, linkage of *discours*, that is, when a hidden actor speaks to another.

While many of the authors of seventeenth-century France expressed themselves about what is proper in the theater and what is not, the important questions are encompassed with differing opinions in the works by Corneille and d'Aubignac. Though theoretical works and critical writings on art may be very important in understanding the plays of this period, the actual works in which the theories are demonstrated or developed probably exert a more direct influence on contemporary authors. Approximately a thousand plays were written and produced during those seventy years, for theater was the most widespread and the most popular art form in the Baroque era.[46] Private performances were held in the various courts, the established companies performed the works in public, and the people came night after night, often to the same play, thus demonstrating the appeal of the *katharsis* which Corneille did not understand fully. The vogue of various genres changed constantly. *Pastorale* was followed by *tragédie,* then *tragi-comédie, comédie-heroïque, tragi-comédie-pastorale,* and at the mid-point of the century, Spanish drama came to the fore. Though there were as few truly great dramatists as there are in any given time or place, there were a great many respectable playwrights, one of whom, De Visé, founded the *Mercure galant,* in which descriptions and criticisms of theatrical productions abound. The typical organization of the professional companies of actors was such that several of them, to increase their incomes, tried their hands at writing, particularly in the comic vein. Plays by actors tend to disregard the rules and unities, and such comedies are often cast in a single act.[47]

In general, it can be said of tragedy, comedy, and pastorale, that after an early period in which they shared many of the same characteristics with most of the rules being applied indifferently to all three, tragedy became the most respected form and that in which the rules were most rigidly applied. The pastorale died out slowly, never completely of course, but shepherds and shepherdesses along with their love intrigues and the sylvan gods and goddesses had less and less appeal to the sophisticated audiences of the courts of Louis XIII and XIV.

Molière and His Influence

It is still possible to argue the various points of excellence in the dramas of Corneille and Racine, placing now one, now the other in first place, but in the comic genre there is one name that stands high above all the rest--Molière. Of all playwrights save possibly Philippe Quinault, who actually wrote the libretti for Lully's *tragédies lyriques,* Molière probably exercised the greatest influence on Lully. They collaborated first in the production of the *ballets de cour* and festivals for Louis XIV and then, together they created the genre, *comédie-ballet.* Both were men of genius, of great humor, and both were quite capable of taking care of themselves in a world in which most men depended on others. Much has been made of the distance which developed between them during the last year of Molière's life with many authors seeing Lully as an ambitious person who simply abandoned Molière and then tried to defeat him completely by limiting the number of musicians who could be used in theatrical productions.

The affair is probably a good deal more complex. In the first place, Molière had his own company which he ran much in the same manner as other professional companies were run. Lully played roles as a member of that company in the royal performances, and he wrote both words and music to some of the songs used in Molière's plays. In what manner was he paid for these services? Did he appear only in the performances given for the king, or was he a part of the company itself, and, if so, how was he paid, for his name does not figure in that capacity in the *Registre La Grange*. It seems quite likely that he was poorly paid, if at all, for his musical contributions. Meanwhile, the plays, once presented at court, were then produced for the public still using Lully's music. If, in addition to this, he acted in them without benefit of being a member of the company and therefore being unable to share the profits from the price of admission, then there was a background of several years during which Lully must have felt that he was not receiving his due. Little actually is known since Lully and Molière had yet another trait in common: they did not talk much about their personal affairs.

Whatever the motivation, there are a few facts to be recorded. The collaboration of Molière and Lully dated from 1659 when *Les Précieuses ridicules* was presented at the Petit-Bourbon with incidental music by Lully. Both men were successfully independent of each other, Molière in the writing of comedy and Lully especially in the composition of ballet in collaboration with the poet, Benserade. In 1671 Lully borrowed 11,000 livres from Molière to help with the construction of the Hôtel de Lully. He appears to have become less active as an associate of Molière during the negotiations by which he acquired the patent for the opera and during the production of the first work given by the Académie. This work was a *pastiche* put together in haste by Quinault mostly drawing on works Lully had written with Molière. As a portion of the patent for the *Académie* Lully asked that the number of musicians to be used by other theaters be reduced. This could have been aimed either at the people who were trying to prevent him from registering the patent or at preventing Molière's company from continuing to make its profits from works which Lully had written. In any case Molière went to the king and got a partial restitution of the right to use musicians in the theaters. In 1672 Molière asked Marc-Antoine Charpentier to re-set *Le*

Mariage forcé, a *comédie-ballet* originally the fruit of Molière's collaboration with Lully. Charpentier wrote the music for *Le Malade imaginaire*.[48] During a performance of this work on February 17, 1673, Molière was taken ill and died shortly afterwards. Since his group no longer had a leader, Louis XIV gave the theater of the Palais-Royal (formerly the palace of the Cardinal Richelieu whose theater had become the home for the troupe of Molière) to the *Académie Royale*. Lully paid his debt to Molière's widow in full within the year.

It would seem that the difference of opinion between the two "grands Baptistes" as they were called, came about as the result of a struggle for power. In justice to both men it should be noted that there cannot be two leaders in an hierarchical system and neither Molière nor Lully was made to bow before another man. Molière was ten years older than Lully. He was independent of royal patronage for his living, while Lully was very much a part of court life. Molière's company produced his own plays, his actors and actresses were trained by him and dependent on him, he owned the sets of the plays and the costumes and machinery as well. Molière received one-half share of the profits once expenses were deducted, and the rest went to the actors and actresses according to ancient rules.[49] In this way Molière had become a prosperous man, and if the structure of his company is compared with that which Lully used in the opera and the *Académie*, the likeness is striking. The greatest difference lies in the fact that Lully's position as director is guaranteed by a royal charter giving him complete authority in organizing the royal Academy. Lully hired a poet, where Molière had hired a musician, and Lully himself supervised the rehearsals, the training of actors and actresses, staging, costumes, sets, and machines in the same manner that Molière had regulated these things in his company. Furthermore, Lully claimed sets, machines, and costumes as personal property, and they account for the greater portion of the wealth he left at his death.[50] The fact is that there cannot be two heads in such an organization. Lully wanted his own company for the same reasons Molière had wanted his, and both men succeeded. Since their active collaboration followed the consolidation of the genre *ballet de cour*, it will be treated later.

The Machine Play and the *Ballet de Cour*

Two other theatrical forms in France were particularly important in their influence on the *tragédie lyrique*: the machine play and the *ballet de cour*. The machine play was evolved from the *tragédie*. As the observance of unity of place became more and more strict, the actual stage settings of *tragédies* became less important, and the spectacular side of drama, the visual appeal, was neglected. The element of the supernatural, of miraculous movements through the air of chariots, clouds, gods, and goddesses had also been banished from the *tragédie*. Though the *tragédie* gained in plausibility, it lost something of popular appeal. The insistence on the use of the Alexandrian couplet to imitate the classical Greek meter also tended to cause a certain uniformity when unbroken by songs and sequences using other line lengths and rhyme schemes. A void was left, and it was filled by the machine play. The machine play is a serious drama in which the spectacular and the marvelous are stressed. It features miraculous machines which permit actors and actresses to seem to fly through the air. Scenery is very elaborate and changes are frequent. The subject is mythological with gods and goddesses and demi-gods playing important roles. There is a prologue, and frequently meters other than the Alexandrian are used. Machine plays contain scenes in recitative, musical episodes and spectacular *divertissements* with ballet which are connected with the main subject. References to Louis XIV and to peace are frequent. Unity of time is observed for the most part, and linkage of scenes is observed. Unity of action and unity of place are usually not respected. Violent and comic scenes are not excluded. Finally, the term "machine play" is not used as strictly as other generic terms. It refers to the predominant emphasis rather than to a specific type of play so that a *pastorale-héroïque* can perfectly well be a machine play at the same time. Also, some plays which made large use of machines were not necessarily dubbed machine plays due to the predominance of drama elements or of ballet.[51]

The *ballet de cour* was a form of court entertainment which developed slowly and combined French royal entertainments with the Italian *mascherate*. Catherine de' Medici did much to promote the genre and brought musicians, dancers, and the customs of her native Florence to France with her when she married Henri II on October 28, 1533. A great number of poets and musicians collaborated in the production of festivals given by the Valois kings, and the political purpose behind such celebrations was only thinly disguised: the glorification of the members of the royal family in the personages of mythology or in allegorical scenes. The famous *Circé, ou le ballet comique de la royne* was produced at Catherine's command in 1581 by Balthazar Beaujoyeulx. This work is composed of long dialogues which are interrupted by ballet *entrées*, or choruses, and is distinguished from other dances and ballets of the time in that it has a story which is followed throughout. The performance lasted from ten o'clock at night until half-past three the following morning and featured a final presentation of gifts as its last ballet. The members of the royal family themselves danced and appeared on stage as was an Italian custom. This was adopted by the French and eventually became a right assured by the patent for the establishment of the *Académie*. *Circé* was but a portion of a festival lasting three days. The ballet was to have ended with a nautical festival in which many mechanical fishes and sea monsters were to have astonished the audience. However, the mechanisms failed to function, and the monsters were left standing close to the settings of *Circé*. The entire festival ended with a grand display of fireworks. In the midst of this demonstration of royal greatness, the sea monsters caught fire which quickly spread to the stage settings, and the whole affair went up in flames. This was not, however, the end of the *ballet de cour*, for *Circé* began a tradition in ballet and music which would resound throughout the history of opera and ballet.[52]

Henry IV loved dancing and during his reign the festivals continued. His marriage by proxy to Marie de' Medici in 1600 in Florence led indirectly to the Paris production in 1604 of *Euridice* for the actual nuptials of the royal pair. This work consisted of music by both Peri and Caccini to the libretto of Rinuccini.[53] Henri IV also brought Italian comedy to Paris, both the *commedia dell'arte* and the written comedy as performed by the troupe of Giovanni Andreini. Plays with music, ballet, and scenic effects were produced from 1603 to 1622 under Andreini's direction, and the introduction of machines and spectacular scenery by the Italians became a feature both of *ballet de cour* and of the opera.[54]

The *ballets de cour* and the court festivals were continued under Louis XIII with the encouragement and the support of Richelieu, together with the exchange of ideas on theater and music between French and Italian authors and composers. Not only does the correspondence between the French Mersenne and the Italian Doni bear witness to this,[55] but also there was a consistent and constant exchange of artists. Louis XIII sent his singer, Pierre de Nyert (who later was to sign Lully's marriage certificate) to study in Rome. On his return, Nyert, with Michel Lambert (Lully's future father-in-law) and Benigne de Bacilly attempted to make a fusion of the two styles of singing with a specific emphasis on enunciation and phrasing as well as on the ornamentation of the doubles.

When Louis XIII married Anne of Austria on January 29, 1617 there was an immense celebration including the performance of the *Déliverance de Renaud* on which the composers Pierre Guédron, Antoine Boësset, and Gabrielle Bataille collaborated. There was a chorus of sixty-four voices and an orchestra of twenty-eight violins and fourteen lutes. Louis XIII was not content merely to watch and to dance ballet. He also designed settings, arranged dance steps, and wrote scenarios and music. During the lifetime of the Duc de Luynes (who directed many productions for Louis XIII) the *ballets de cour* were based on a continuous story. Towards the end of the King's reign, however, there was a return to the *ballet à entrées*, that is, a ballet with a general theme. The machines were produced by the Italian, Francini, one of whose descendants became *maître d'hôtel* to Louis XIV and married Lully's eldest daughter.

This tradition was continued during the minority of Louis XIV. There were many collaborators in these productions. The *inventeur* laid out the general plan, the poet rhymed the *récits* which introduced each *entrée* and which appeared between the last *entrée* and the *Grand Ballet* which was danced by members of the royal family and the nobility. The poet also wrote a *livret* which was distributed to the public and contained not only identification of roles and the words to the *récits* but also some interesting comments on the private lives and habits of the actual persons dancing each part. The public was not a paying public but rather the *grand peuple* who was admitted to witness the frolicking of their royal masters free of charge. Just as later thousands would march past the solitary table at which Louis XIV sat taking his meals to the accompaniment of his musicians, thousands came to watch both the participants and the royal and semiroyal audiences of the *ballet de cour*.[56]

Lully entered the King's service in 1652 as a dancer and composer of instrumental music. The occupations of violinist and choreographer often were combined since as dancer, he would arrange the steps of the ballet, and as musician, he would compose the music. The most brilliant of such French artists of the time were Bocan, Beauchamp (later the choreographer of the *Académie royale*), Dumanoir, and Lully himself. The character of the dances is illustrated by engravings which can be seen in the Louvre, the Bibliothèque Nationale, and several other public and private libraries. From these, it can be seen that the geometric figures of the ballets of the previous century have been replaced by dances of action and pantomime. The main composers of instrumental music for the ballets at this time were Michel Mazuel (head of the twenty-four violins of the King), Lazarin (whose post of composer of instrumental music became Lully's), Dumanoir, and Constantin (who later became head of the twenty-four). The composers of vocal music were Cambefort, Jean Boësset, François Chancy, and Paul Auger.

The first ballet for the King in which Lully appeared was the *Ballet de la Nuit*. Jean de Cambefort wrote all of the *récits* for this work. According to Henry Prunières,

> Son récit de la Nuit apparaît comme un prototype du récitatif lulliste
> par l'insistance avec laquelle il emploie le rhythme dactylique, par
> son respect de la césure et de la rime, et aussi par certaines

tournures mélodiques. Le récit de Venus: Fuyez bien loin, d'une allure dégagée et vive, est déjà dans la manière de Lully.[57]

His *récit de la Nuit* seems to be a prototype of the Lully recitative because of the extensive use of dactylic rhythm, the respect for caesura and rhyme and also certain melodic traits. The *récit de Venus*, "*Fuyez bien loin*," with its free and lively pace, is already written in the manner of Lully.

In 1654 Lully appeared with Michel Lambert and Beauchamp in three ballets, the *Ballet des Proverbes*, the *Ballet du Temps*, and the ballets interpolated into Carlo Caproli's *Noces de Pélée et de Thétis*. Unfortunately, the music by Caproli has been lost, but the libretto by the Abbé Buti, and the verses to the ballets by Benserade show that the work was conceived as a whole on the same subject. It has often been remarked that Lully danced several roles in this work at the side of the young King, but little has been made of the fact that this was, to our certain knowledge,[58] the first opera which Lully saw, and that the ballets within it were not *intermèdes*, unconnected with the action, but rather a true portion of the play. The "*Air pour l'Esté et ses suivants*" from the *Ballet du Temps* is by Lully and resembles those of his French contemporaries in form and melodic contour.

From this time until the King stopped dancing and therefore no longer required his musicians to present him with ballets, Lully was active both as a composer and as a dancer. At first, he collaborated with other composers, just as Benserade shared the task of writing verses with other authors, but from 1658 until the founding of the opera in 1672 almost all of the great ballets were by Lully and Benserade.

Lully collaborated in the writing of two ballets in 1655, the *Ballet des Plaisirs* and the *Ballet des Bienvenus*. The "Serenade" from the *Ballet des Plaisirs* presents some of the features which will be typical of the Lully recitative: several changes of meter and tempo within sections, and the last line of the poetry repeated with a different musical setting.[59]

The ballet *Psyché* and *La Galanterie du Temps* were presented in 1656. A copy of the libretto of the latter is in the Bibliothèque du Conservatoire, but the music is lost. According to Prunières, all of the airs are in Italian, and the vocal part is quite extensive. It was in this production that the *seize petits violons* made their first appearance and Loret in the *Muze historique* comments favorably on the new group. Lully imposed a style of playing ornaments which was in opposition to the florid improvisations of the *24 violons du roi*. He insisted that ornaments be played only where they are marked or in pieces written in slow tempo such as elegies.[60]

The *Ballet de l'Amour malade* was presented on January 17, 1657. It is a little opera combined with a ballet. The words are by Abbé Buti, and the music by Lully appears in his complete works. The French air, "*Que les jaloux sont importuns,*" very much resembles the songs which Lully later interpolated into scenes written in dialogue. There are no meter changes such as are found in those vocal compositions which are marked RECIT and which are typical of the Lully recitative in the *tragédie lyrique*. One of the *entrées* of the *Ballet de l'Amour malade* is a scene for "*onze Docteurs qui reçoivent un Docteur en Asnerie.*" One of the doctors, Scaramouche, was played by Lully himself. Benserade, in his written commentary, says,

> Aux plus sçavans docteurs je sçay faire la loye
> Ma grimace vaut mieux que tout leur préambule
> Scaramouche en effet n'est pas si ridicule
> Et si Scaramouche que moy.[61]

> To the most learned doctors I can dictate the law
> My grimace is worth more than all their preambles
> Scaramouche in effect is not as ridiculous
> or as Scaramouche as I.

The idea is daring. The troupe of Tiberio Fiorilli, the real Scaramouche, was in Paris at the time, and the character he had invented was that of a braggart and imposter who made his way through life by the use of his wits, with many disguises, playing all parts, but a man whose real heart, under his buffoonery and effrontery, is known to none but himself. Lully was already calling himself "de" Lully but he played Scaramouche more than once in the ballets. Fifteen years after the appearance of the *Ballet de l'Amour malade*, Molière wrote a scene similar to the scene of the *docteurs en Asnerie* for the *Malade imaginaire*.

The following is a list of the ballets written principally by Lully and Benserade between 1658 and 1669.

Ballet d'Alcidiane, February 14, 1658
Ballet de la Raillerie, February 19, 1659
Ballet de l'Impatience, February 19, 1661
Ballet des Saisons, July 25, 1661
Ballet des Arts, January 8, 1663
Ballet des Noces de Village, October 3, 1663
Ballet des Amours déguisés, February 13, 1664
Ballet de la naissance de Venus, January 26, 1665
Ballet des Gardes, June 1665 (No words.)

Ballet des Muses, December 2, 1666
Ballet de Flore, February 13, 1669

Prunières compares the airs Lully wrote in Italian with those he wrote in French for the *Ballet d'Alcidiane* and says that Lully's Italian airs are filled with melodic devices which are very French, while there are few Italianate traits in the French airs. The latter are quite in the tradition of Antoine Boësset and differ very little from those written by Michel Lambert and le Camus at about the same time.[62] The main differences which Lully has made between the *récits* in the two languages are the vocalizations on a single syllable in the Italian *récits* and the meter changes in the French *récits*. Both French and Italian *récits* contain instances of the last line of poetry being repeated with different music (both melody and rhythm), and both feature a melodic style of writing with no instances of *parlando*. All are in two parts with repetitions indicated and most of them are strophic. In addition to the contrasted French and Italian styles of the *récits*, Lully has written two marches, the *Marche Italienne* and the *Marche Françoise*, which follows immediately. The most obvious difference is the rhythmic pattern which characterizes each of these dances. Lully underlined the contrast between the two styles even further in 1659 with the dialogue between Italian and French music in the *Ballet de la Raillerie* in which each side, after presenting its virtues, decides that they should live in harmony instead of disputing supremacy. (As noted above, *Les Précieuses ridicules* also appeared in 1659 with incidental music by Lully.)

Descriptions of the performances of the ballets are to be found in *Le Ballet de cour de Louis XIV* by Marie-Françoise Christout but the music is not readily available. A few are to be found in Lully's complete works. A full study of the manuscripts should be made to discover to what extent music from one ballet was repeated in another. It is known that this was a common practice, for the King frequently asked to have an entertainment at a moment's notice so that Lully developed a repertory of *intermèdes*, love-dialogues, and pastoral sequences. He also had a repertory of ballet *entrées* featuring hunters, satyrs, Turks, demons, beggars, astrologists, wild spirits, zephyrs, peasants, Spaniards, and gypsies, all ready to be incorporated into a presentation.[63] Molière's *Ballet des Ballets* is such a work, as the title indicates, and it is well known that the various *fêtes* and *grottes* de Versailles contained excerpts from a variety of other works. Such was the process of adding ballets to Cavalli's *Xerxes*.

Two Italian Operas in Paris

Cardinal Mazarin had commissioned Cavalli to write an opera to a libretto by the Abbé Buti, *Ercole amante*, for the marriage of Louis XIV. Cavalli did not finish the work in time, and, on the insistence of the Cardinal, he decided to present a revival of *Xerxes*, first produced in Venice in 1654. Cavalli eliminated the choruses from this work, simplified the action, and reorganized it into five acts from the original three. To ensure the approval of the French public, Mazarin asked Lully to supply ballets between the acts, but at such short notice it was necessary to use *intermèdes* from previous productions bearing no relationship whatsoever to the opera. There are six altogether.

1. Basques dressed in costumes which are divided down the middle, half-French, half-Spanish.

2. Peasants singing and dancing in the Spanish style.

3. Scaramouche, disguised in a crowd of doctors, is recognized and chased away (Lully again played Scaramouche).

4. A ship-owner with his slaves who carry monkeys dressed as clowns accompanied by sailors playing on "trompettes marines."

5. Clowns.

6. The triumph of Bacchus.

Due to the short notice, all of the parts were taken by professional dancers with Lully dancing the leading roles himself.[64]

Ercole amante was at last presented on February 7, 1662. Furnished with a prologue in praise of Louis XIV, supplied with ballets and spectacles, and given settings and machines, it comes very close to being a machine play. It is a serious drama on a mythological subject, and it has a topical prologue in which the marriage of Louis XIV and Marie-Thérèse cements peace between Spain and France. There are comic elements and, above all, the principal importance has been given to spectacle, for there are violent storms, flying chariots, magic spells, ghosts, a ship sunk in a storm at sea, a cemetery scene, a funeral procession, and at last the cloud-palace descends with the Royal Family.

A new stage had been constructed in the Tuileries by Le Vau, d'Orbay, and Vigarani for this performance. The machines had been perfected laboriously over a two-year period by Gasparo Vigarani and his two sons, Carlo and Lodovico. Christout suggests that the new stage, of extraordinary proportions, was perhaps responsible for the fact that the voices of the Italian singers were obscured by the sounds of the machines. The libretto, again by the Abbé Buti, was confusing and filled with a myriad of details which have little bearing on the main story; however, as in his libretto for Caproli, the Abbé gave pretexts for the ballets and connected them with the story. Ballets take place at the end of each act, and the final *grand divertissement* contains twenty-six *entrées*. All of the ballets were by Lully. As with *Xerxes*, the French newspaper accounts praised the ballets while finding the opera very long, and everyone marveled at the machines. Vigarani produced a great palace, resting on a cloud, and the whole Royal Family descended to earth in it to dance the grand ballet after which they were again swept up into the heavens.[65]

In spite of the popularity of machine plays, *Ercole amante* had only limited success. The music passed with very little notice, while the spectacles and ballets were highly praised. Cavalli and his company of Italians had taken all the major parts except for two, those sung by Mademoiselle Hilaire (Dupuy) and Mademoiselle de la Barre.[66] The Italian singers were overbearing in their conduct towards their French colleagues, and the relations between French and Italian musicians were strained. The story was too complicated to cause suspense and too far-fetched to provoke the admiration of reason. In short, the major elements necessary to a successful theatrical production had been overlooked. The music of the opera proper was in the Italian mode rather than the French, and this was a touchy question several years before Cavalli came to Paris as shown, for example, in the dialogue of the *Ballet de la Raillerie*. The story was similar to those found in Venetian opera and the Italian pastorale, while the French had become accustomed either to the simple, clearly outlined plots of the *ballet de cour* or the driving and concise structure of the classical tragedy. Only the machines and the ballet were within their experience, and, as should have been expected, these were what received praise.

The next work commanded by Louis XIV was the *Ballet des Arts*, 1663, by Lully, with the assistance of Michel Lambert (now his father-in-law), Benserade, and the choreographers Beauchamp, Vertpré, and Dolivet. Carlo Vigarani, Lully's future partner, created the settings and machines. All the *récits* are in French and were sung by French artists. Loret, in the *Muze historique* says that the ballet was worthy of the gods and that never had there been such dancing, while giving special praise to

. . .la parfaite symphonie
Dont Baptiste, esprit transcendant,
Estoit Chef et Surintendant.[67]

The *ballet de cour* and the French *récit* won the approval of critics, royalty, nobility, and public over the attempted importation of Italian opera because they responded to French taste.

The *Comédies Ballets*

The *comédies ballets* which Lully wrote with Molière are the most immediate and most important predecessors of the *tragédie lyrique*. In these works Lully perfected the art of portraying character and advancing action, for he not only provided music for ballet scenes but also set a lot of dialogue.

While many literary critics deplore the time Molière spent writing court festivals, the fact remains that the works produced by Molière and Lully from 1664 to 1671 contain some of the author's finest comedies.

Le Mariage forcé, 1664
Les Plaisirs de l'Ile enchantée, 1664 (containing la Princesse d'Elide, les Fâcheux, the first three acts of Tartuffe, and le Mariage forcé)
L'Amour médicin, 1665
La Pastorale comique, 1667
Le Sicilien, 1667
Les Fêtes de Versailles (George Dandin) 1668
Monsieur de Pourceaugnac, 1669
Les Amants magnifiques, 1670
Le Bourgeois gentilhomme, 1670
Psyché (with the collaboration of Pierre Corneille and songs by Quinault) 1671

Concerning the collaboration of Molière and Lully, Prunières calls attention to several things which cast doubt on the opinion often held that the great Molière was used by Lully as a stepping stone to a high position.[68] In the first place, there is a great contrast between the social status of the two men. Molière spent much of his early life wandering and in the company of players, while Lully spent his youth at the courts of Mademoiselle de Montpensier and Louis XIV. Molière appears as a pensioner of the King in Colbert's accounts, while Lully does not. The King and his court did not attend Molière's wedding, nor did Louis XIV sign Molière's wedding certificate. Lully held many offices in the court, including that of *surintendant* which he already possessed in 1662, while Molière never held an equivalent position although Racine and Boileau both became court historians.   Apart from the social question, Lully was in charge of the performing forces of the court, both instrumental and vocal, before the two men began to collaborate actively. In short, it seems clear that Molière did not raise Lully to a position of eminence at court, since Lully was the person who held the position of power from the beginning of the association of the two men.

The works produced by Molière and Lully fall into two distinct types: machine plays and *comédies-ballets*. The machine plays make use of shepherds and shepherdesses, and when the music of the *comédies-ballets* is in the form of *intermèdes* rather than being a part of the drama, the plot is also based on pastoral themes. *La Princesse d'Elide, la Pastorale comique, les Fêtes de Versailles* (the *intermèdes* for *Georges Dandin*), *les Amants magnifiques,* and *Psyché* are machine plays because of their magnificence although the first four are pastorales. *Le Mariage forcé, l'Amour médecin, le Sicilien, Monsieur de Pourceaugnac,* and *le Bourgeois gentilhomme* differ from the machine plays in that comedy is freshly invented, and the musical sections are completely integrated into the drama, while the settings play a secondary role. The machine plays were produced for the King and his court, while the *comédies-ballets,* after first appearing before the King, were played by Molière's company at the Palais-Royal.

Both types provided Lully with the proving ground necessary for perfecting his craft and while the machine plays lead directly to the opera as Prunières says,[69] the *comédies-ballets* provided Lully with the opportunity to experiment with the portrayal of character and action. In the machine plays the types of scenes which Lully had written for the *ballets de cour* are found, but they have been developed and polished. They form the link between the style of the *ballet de cour* and the *tragédies lyriques*. The explanatory *récit* which headed each section of the *ballet de cour* was adopted and, as in the *ballet de cour,* it has formal structure and is strophic although the repetitions are written out. An example is the monologue of Cloris from *le Grand Divertissement de Versailles*.[70] Like the *récits* from the *ballet de cour,* it contains frequent meter changes and the melody is songlike in style. It begins with a *ritournelle* scored for two violins and the continuo, and there is a second *ritournelle* which interrupts the *récit*. The dramatic purpose of this monologue is to inform the audience that the shepherd whom Cloris loved, but spurned, is dead. This form of recitative appears in the *tragédie lyrique,* notably the great monologue of *Armide,* "*Enfin il est en mon pouvoir,*" and the mad scene from *Roland*.

There is an example of dialogue in the same work from which it is but a step to numerous similar scenes in the *tragédies lyriques.* Two shepherds insist that they love two shepherdesses, while the latter have no intention of listening to such nonsense. The musical setting contains frequent meter changes, some use of *parlando* mixed with a more melodic style of writing, and there is repetition of a line of poetry with a completely new musical setting. The two shepherds often speak together as do the two shepherdesses, but the scene, cast in recitative style throughout, is never a duet or quartet.[71] The *"Dépit amoureux"* from *les Amants magnifiques* is an example of a dialogue scene which begins in *parlando* style but which becomes more and more lyrical and culminates in a song.

The final grand ballet of *Georges Dandin* is a good example of the scene-complex wherein recitative, song, ballet, and choral episodes are mixed. In this particular instance, the scene begins with an orchestral *rondeau* followed by two songs. There is a short dialogue in which it is explained that Love and the god of Love are the strongest of all forces. The troupe of Bacchus enters and presents the joys of their god and of wine. A battle ensues with recited shouts, choral exclamations, solo passages, a section in contrapuntal style, and finally the combatants are apostrophized to make peace, there being no conflict between the complementary pleasures of love and wine.[72] The differentiation between the musical styles of song, recitative, choral passages in recitative, and chorale is clear-cut. The meter changes which are so frequent in recitative are absent in the songs where the melodic structure is simple and folk-like. The recitative can be written either in a *parlando* style with the use of outlined triads and repeated notes, or in a more lyrical manner, which, due to the meter changes, never quite becomes song. The choral passages are interrupted by shouts and exclamations, and the section in contrapuntal style portrays the confusion of battle between the two choirs so that the final passage, which is sung by all, represents musically the unity called for by the words.

While these are the three types of scenes in which recitative is developed through the ballet and *comédie-ballet* it should be noted that the structure of scenes, as well as the over-all structure of the *tragédie lyrique* grows directly from these works. Since scenes are constructed according to the characters on stage in French theater, the same practice was adopted for the *tragédie lyrique.* The monologue, *récit* of the *ballet de cour,* is a scene; a dialogue, a scene-complex, a trio, or a song (each of which was an *intermède* in a *comédie-ballet,* or an *entrée* in a *ballet de cour*) became an entire scene in the *tragédie lyrique* regardless of its length or structure. Were it not for Quinault's skill at linking scenes, continuity would be lacking and, even with that skill, previous knowledge of the plot is often necessary for the audience to follow the action.

In drama of this type the delineation of character is very important, and it is from Molière in the *comédies-ballets* that Lully learned this art. In *Le Mariage forcé*, Sganarelle consults a magician to determine whether or not, if he takes the extreme step of getting married, his young wife will cuckold him. The magician gives no real answer, though it is intimated that Sganarelle's fears are well founded. Throughout the scene, Sganarelle speaks his lines while the magician sings--adding not a little to the old man's frustration. There may have been a practical reason for the partial setting to music of this scene. Molière played his own leading roles and he was not a singer. Other examples of musical characterization are to be found throughout the *comédies-ballets*: the scene of the two Italian doctors--one of whom was played by Lully while Molière was Pourceaugnac--attempting to give a purge to Pourceaugnac, the scene of the two lawyers expounding on the evils of polygamy wherein one speaks very slowly and the other very rapidly (the message is the same: *la polygamie est une offense pendable*), and the whole series of scenes in *Le Bourgeois gentilhomme* culminating in the finale in which Jourdain-Molière is made a Turkish gentleman by Mamamouchi-Lully. Deserving of special mention are the two songs from the singing lesson in this drama. The singing teacher composes a love song on stage (with a number of interludes for writing and thinking aloud) and then sings it to his master. Mr. Jourdain, however, prefers what he calls a more emotional song which he sings without accompaniment. The second song is an excellent example of how not to set French words to music, for the melodic stresses are so placed as to make a grotesque effect through the prolongation of syllables and words. What with the necessity for composing music for ballet *entrées* of all varieties and the settings of songs and dialogue in the *comédies-ballets*, Lully acquired a high degree of experience in portrayal of character and in writing music for dialogues, monologues, and spectacular scenes.

In the final machine play, *Psyché*, Lully had three collaborators--Molière, Pierre Corneille, and Philippe Quinault. There has been much speculation as to why Lully chose Quinault, a minor poet, over Molière as his collaborator in the creation of the *tragédie lyrique*. In *Psyché* it was the words to songs which Molière asked Quinault to write, while Corneille completed the drama sketched by Molière. It is a pity that this version of *Psyché* is not readily available in score for comparison with the *tragédie lyrique* of the same name written in 1678. The words of the Italian lament are the same and were probably written by Lully. In any event it can be surmised that it was during this collaboration that Lully became fully aware of Quinault's ability to write verse which, while it does not stand well by itself, is admirably suited to being set to music. Quinault's character was also far better adapted to being a collaborator than Molière's. It should be noted that Lully had written some quite simple recitative for Molière to sing in dialogues, but the protagonist of an opera must be able to sing, and Molière could not. These reasons, added to those of a more practical nature mentioned above, seem more than enough to explain why, when offered a poet whose taste in verse was better suited to musical setting, Lully detached himself from Molière.

The question of the foundation of the *Académie* and the background for the *tragédie lyrique* will be treated in the next chapter as the pastorales of Perrin, Cambert, Guichard, and Sablières did not exercise an artistic influence on the *tragédie lyrique*. The stuff of which the pastorale was made, shepherds and shepherdesses with a plot based on love-tangles, was part of the *ballet de cour*, and Lully was well acquainted with writing such works for he supplied ballet *entrées* dealing with the shepherds in his collaboration with Molière. Indeed, if the *intermèdes* for *Georges Dandin* were played without the intervening acts of the play, the ballet would constitute a pastorale entirely set to music. The style Lully used in writing his ballet *entrées* for both the machine plays of Molière and the *comédies-ballets* clearly shows his development as a dramatic artist. Due to his position as *surintendant*, he, more than any other musician in France, had the musical forces to produce whatever he wished from 1662 to 1672, and he used those years to perfect his style. King Louis XIV gave up dancing when he was thirty-one years old, and thereafter the *ballet de cour* suffered a loss of popularity for it was dependent on the King's patronage and his commands. When Colbert proposed to Lully that he buy Perrin's patent, it represented an opportunity for both financial independence and greater artistic freedom. It was the patent which Lully wanted, not the musical style, for he had developed his own already, one which was imitated by all other composers in France desirous of capturing a bit of royal favor.

Due to his position of complete power in musical matters Lully was able to impose his wishes without opposition on those who worked under him in the creation of the *Académie* and the opera. He had a highly complex personality, was quick to learn, and assimilated all of his diverse experiences as an artist. His personal style of musical composition was to a large degree the product of his own life, and the choices which he made in giving form to the *tragédie lyrique* cannot be appreciated fully without some knowledge of Lully, himself.

NOTES

[1] In *Cadmus et Hermione*, the Nurse is the typical old woman and the man-servant, Arbas, is a cowardly braggart. In *Alceste* the nymph, Céphise, is the flighty and inconstant girl who plays two lovers off against each other. The father of Admète is a caricature of the doddering old man, while Lychas is the sly lady-killer. In *Isis* the comic scene arises from a situation rather than from characters. Iris and Mercure pretend that they are in love and play a false love-scene.

[2] This is true of all of the *tragédies lyriques* to some extent, but it is particularly striking in regard to secondary characters. The audience is expected to know the "good" characters from the "evil" characters by name alone. The same previous knowledge of plot is expected, for example, when Proserpine must stay in the Underworld for part of each year because she ate six pomegranate seeds. In the *tragédie lyrique* the audience is told only that Proserpine has eaten--not what she ate--and the compromise itself is not explained but rather understood from previous knowledge of the story.

[3] Robert Mantero, ed., *Corneille critique* (Paris: Buchet/Chastel, 1964), pp. 176-77.

[4] Jefferson Butler Fletcher, *Literature of the Italian Renaissance* (New York: The Macmillan Co., 1934), p. 277.

[5] Ibid., p. 278.

[6] Aristotle, *On Poetry and Style*, trans. by G. M. A. Grube (Indianapolis, Indiana: The Bobbs-Merrill Co., Inc., 1958), p. 11.

[7] Ibid., p. 17.

[8] Ibid., p. 24.

[9] Ibid., p. 30.

[10] Ibid., p. 23.

[11] Ibid., p. 36.

[12] Horace, *The Complete Works of Horace*, Intro by John Marshall, trans. by various hands (London and Toronto: J. M. Dent & Sons, Ltd., 1923), p. 139.

[13] Ibid.

[14] Ibid., p. 138.

[15] Ibid.

[16] Ibid., p. 139.

[17] Ibid.

[18] Ibid., p. 135.

[19] Duckworth, in his Introduction to *The Complete Roman Drama*, described the Roman theater. There were no stone theaters at the time of Terence and Plautus, and plays

were acted on a long stage constructed outdoors for the occasion. The stage represented a city street with two or three houses out of which actors entered the scene. Plautus' *The Rope* called for a strip of seacoast with a cottage and a temple in the background. For more, see George E. Duckworth, *The Complete Roman Drama* (New York: Random House, 1942), pp. xxii-xxiv.

[20]Ibid., pp. xxiv-xxvii.

[21]Joseph Spencer Kennard, *The Italian Theater* (New York: William Edwin Rudge, 1932). On pp. 8 and 9 he tells that a live man was ordered crucified and then devoured by a bear.

[22]Duckworth discusses the probability of the performance of Seneca's tragedies in ancient Rome on pages xxxvii and xxxviii.

[23]C. H. C. Wright, *A History of French Literature*, Vol. 1 (New York: Haskell House Publishers, Ltd., 1969), p. 211.

[24]Duckworth, op. cit., p. xxxviii.

[25]In Seneca's *Medea*, the reaction of the chorus is against her, whereas in the *Medea* of Euripides she is treated with more sympathy.

[26]Duckworth, op. cit., p. xi.

[27]Sophonisba, a Carthaginian princess, daughter of Hasdrubal, is taken prisoner by the Romans. She is saved from dishonor and slavery by drinking a cup of poison sent to her by her husband, Masinissa.

[28]Trissino wrote in his "Poetica" of 1549, "I shall not depart from the rules and precepts of the Ancients and especially Aristotle." Quoted by Fletcher, op. cit., p. 280. Cinzio wrote his "Discorso intorno al comporre delle comedie e delle tragedie" between 1543 and 1554. See: P. R. Horne, *The Tragedies of Giambattista Cinthio Giraldi* (London: Oxford University Press, 1962).

[29]Kennard, op. cit., p. 161. The Farnese Theatre in Parma could seat seven thousand.

[30]Ibid., chap. VI, pp. 105-35 and Fletcher, op. cit., p. 283 ff.

[31]For more see Fletcher, op. cit., pp. 289-92.

[32]The pastorale is discussed in Kennard, op. cit., chap. VIII, *passim*; Fletcher, op. cit., pp. 295-97; and Arnold Hartmann Jr., "Battista Guarini and Il Pastor Fido," *The Musical Quarterly*, XXXIX (July, 1953), 424.

[33]All extant plays are listed by Henry Carrington Lancaster, *A History of French Dramatic Literature in the Seventeenth Century* (10 vols.; Baltimore: The Johns Hopkins Press, 1936). The history of the performance of each play is given with its description in the text.

[34]Wright, op. cit., p. 70.

[35]For more: Wright, op. cit., chap. VII, pp. 71-85.

[36]Lancaster, op. cit., part 1, Vol. 2, pp. 747-50.

[37]Ibid., p. 376.

[38]Ibid.

[39]François Hédelin Abbé d'Aubignac, *The Whole Art of the Stage*, anonymous translator (London: 1684, reprinted by New York: Benjamin Blom, Inc., 1968), p. 88.

[40]Claveret's *L'Esprit fort* is an example. It is, according to Lancaster, the earliest case of complete linkage of scenes. See: Lancaster, op. cit., p. 590.

[41]d'Aubignac, op. cit., Book 3, p. 88.

[42]Ibid., p. 90.

[43]Lancaster, op. cit., Part 3, Vol. 1, p. 9.

[44]This summary is taken from the English translation printed in 1684.

[45]The edition of 1660 is in three volumes each of which was introduced by a *Discours*. Manero, in *Corneille critique*, reprints all three with commentaries on the variants made by Corneille for subsequent editions of his works which appeared in 1663, 1668, and 1682.

[46]Lancaster, op. cit., Part 1, Vol. 2, pp. 760-63; Part 2, Vol. 2, pp. 777-81; Part 3, Vol. 2, pp. 863-68.

[47]In addition to his or her quota of the gate, the author received a lump sum for a play. Among actors who wrote at the Hôtel de Bourgogne were: Poisson, Brécourt, Champmeslé and Hauteroche; at the Marais: Chevalier, and Nanteuil who was not connected by contract with a Parisian troupe. See: Lancaster, op. cit., Part 3, Vol. 2, p. 753 ff.

[48]For a description of Charpentier's activities with Molière, see: H. Wiley Hitchcock, "Marc-Antoine Charpentier and the Comédie-Française," *Journal of the American Musicological Society*, XXIV (1971), 255-81.

[49]Lancaster, op. cit., Part 1, Vol. 2, p. 726.

[50]See: Jean Cordey, "Lully d'après l'inventaire de ses biens," *Revue de musicologie*, XXXVII (July, 1935).

[51]Examples of machine plays: Pierre Corneille, *Andromède, la Toison d'or;* Boyer, *la Feste de Venus, Ulysse, les Amours de Jupiter et de Sémélé;* Chapoton, *Orphée et Euridice;* Rotrou, *Deux Sosies;* Gilbert, *Amours de Diane et d'Endimion;* Molière, *Amphitryon;* Molière and P. Corneille, *Psyché;* François Pascal, *Endymion.*

[52]Norman Demuth, *French Opera* (Sussex: The Artemis Press, Ltd., 1963), chap II.. pp. 26-44, *passim.*

[53]For a discussion of the *Euridice* and which portions were by Peri and which by Caccini, see Demuth, op. cit., pp. 46-47.

[54]Ibid., pp. 45-51.

[55]This correspondence can be found in Mersenne, *Correspondance du P. Marin* (9 vols.; Paris: Presses Universitaires de France, 1955; Editions du Centre National de la Recherche Scientifique, 1963 and following).

[56]See: The introductions by Henry Prunières in Jean-Baptiste Lully, *Oeuvres Complètes*, les Ballets, Vols. 1 and 2; Margaret M. McGowan, *L'Art du ballet de cour en France 1581-1643* (Paris: Editions du Centre National de la Recherche Scientifique, 1963), and Marie-Françoise Christout, Le Ballet de cour de Louis XIV, 1643-1672 (Paris: Editions A. et J. Picard & Cie., 1967).

[57]Lully, *Oeuvres Complètes*, ed. Henry Prunières, les Ballets, I (Paris: Editions de la Revue Musicale, 1931), p. xvii.

[58]Lully had been in France a little over a year when Luigi Rossi's *Orfeo* was produced in 1647, for which reason Prunières surmised that Lully saw it.

[59]Lully, les Ballets, Vol. 1, pp. 9-11.

[60]Ibid., p. xix.

[61]Ibid., Vol. 2, p. 41.

[62]Ibid., p. xi.

[63]Lully, *Oeuvres Complètes*, les Comédies-Ballets, Vol. 1, p. ix.

[64]Lully, les Ballets, Vol. 2, p. xiii. See also, Christout, op. cit., pp. 101-103.

[65]Christout, op. cit., pp. 106-108.

[66]See Demuth, op. cit., for the cast of singers, p. 87; and Christout, op. cit., pp. 128-264, for the names of the dancers of the ballets.

[67]Quoted in Christout, op. cit., p. 109.

[68]Lully, *les Comédies-Ballets*, Vol. 1, pp. vi-vii.

[69]Ibid., Vol. 2, p. xii.

[70]Ibid., pp. 171-78.

[71]Ibid., pp. 160-70.

[72]Ibid., pp. 180-223.

CHAPTER II

BIOGRAPHICAL SKETCH OF JEAN-BAPTISTE DE LULLY

Lully left very few records of his life, though he lived in an age when many people were writing profusely about themselves in letters and diaries. There are bills of sale signed by him and accounts of his rental property, but even manuscripts in his hand are so rare that the single sheet found by Prunières was considered to be a major discovery.[1] It is possible to determine where Lully was and what he was doing through the lists of his performances at court and the date of the productions of his works. Other sources are newspaper accounts and letters written by opera lovers. He was involved in two lengthy court cases the briefs of which constitute another source of information. What should have been last, however, was usually taken first by writers, namely, the satirical songs, anecdotes, and early biographical writings. The first of the biographies was written in 1704,[2] that is, seventeen years after his death; and while the details concerning his appearance, manner of working, rehearsing, and producing his operas are lively and picturesque, so many of them have been proved to be false that doubt is cast on the entire work.

Mention of Lully is made in nearly all histories of music, works on opera, and encyclopedias, and there are numerous articles most of which are based on early and unreliable sources. While as many of these works as possible have been examined, every effort has been made in the present biographical sketch to present only that which is supported by actual documents or by strong, circumstantial evidence with the objective of presenting a man, not a legend.

Origins, Early Life, and Entrance into the King's Service

Jean-Baptiste Lully was baptized on November 29, 1632, at San Giovanni Battista, in Florence. He was the son of Lorenzo Lulli and Caterina di Gabriello del Sera of the parish, Santa Lucia sul Prato.[3] Henry Prunières found the marriage certificate, dated February 16, 1620, in the registry of the church, *San Salvatore degl'Ognissanti*, which had been collected with those of other churches in the Archbishopric of Florence. This document clearly states that Lorenzo Lulli was a miller and that his wife, Caterina, was the daughter of a miller.[4]

Since there were families of noble origins who were called both Lulli and del Sera in Florence at the time of Lully's birth, he took advantage of the equivocal situation when he went to France and claimed noble origin for himself. His papers of naturalization show no trace of noble birth except for the use of the particule, "*de*".[5] However, on his wedding certificate he boldy signed himself: "Jean Baptiste de Lully, escuyer, fils de Laurent de Lully, gentilhomme Florentin, et de deffunte damoiselle Catherine del Sera."[6] It was not the truth, but he defended it staunchly, so that intensive research was necessary to prove its inaccuracy. His parents' marriage certificate and his baptismal certificate are the only records which we have of Lully before he came to France.

There is a brief mention of Lully in the *Mémoires* of Mademoiselle de Montpensier according to which she requested her cousin, Roger de Lorraine, Chevalier de Guise, to bring her an Italian boy on his return from the Island of Malta so that she might learn the language through conversation.[7] The keeper of the archives of the order of the Knights of Malta wrote to Henry Prunières that there is no record of Roger de Lorraine ever having set foot on the island. However, there is a lengthy correspondence between Barducci, the Florentine representative in France, and the court of the Grand Duke Ferdinand II according to which Roger de Lorraine passed through Florence in February of the year 1646. In March, he was seen riding through the streets of Paris in the coach of Mademoiselle de Montpensier. It seems probable that he brought Lully to France with him at that time.[8]

Lully probably was connected with some court in Florence as it was the custom then for talented young men to be cultivated and educated as soon as they showed special aptitude. In addition to this probability, Lully wrote on his marriage certificate that his mother was dead (and there is no reason to doubt this) making it even more likely that the father would have sought to place the boy at court. When Roger de Lorraine requested a young man to converse in Italian with his cousin, he would have been well aware that a boy with musical talent and the beginning of instruction would be highly valued.

Who could have recommended the young Lully? There are two possibilities: Ferdinand II, himself, or Charles de Lorraine, father of Roger, who had been living in Florence since 1631 when he had been exiled from France due to the consanguinity of the houses of Guise and Bourbon. Either man could have recommended the boy and if, as seems to be probable, Lully's family were broken, he would have been greatly tempted by the opportunity.

There are no documents concerning Lully from 1646 to 1652, the date his name first appears as *garçon de chambre* at 150 livres a year on the accounts of Mademoiselle de Montpensier.[9] Her accounts from 1644 to 1652 were destroyed in the *Fronde*, that series of revolts of the aristocracy against the crown during the regency of Anne of Austria. Such boys had few duties other than waiting on the pleasure of their patrons while receieving training in courtly manners and life. Mademoiselle de Montpensier was not only the daughter of Gaston d'Orléans, and a cousin of the King, but she also was an ardent patron of the arts. She lived at the Tuileries and organized a social season filled with concerts, plays, and balls. She had her own theatrical company, maintained a band of six violinists, and had, amongst her pensioners, the singers, Michel Lambert and his sister-in-law, Hilaire DuPuy.[10]

Michel Lambert, called "the new Orpheus," was a composer of *airs de cour* as well as a singer, and his services were in demand at Mademoiselle's court, at that of the king, and other houses of the nobility. He was a teacher of singing and took a prominent part in the production of *ballets de cour*. His sister-in-law, Hilaire DuPuy, was a fine enough singer that when Cambert was sent to England in 1673 to organize an academy like that of Lully's, Hilaire DuPuy went with him.[11]

Though evidence is purely circumstantial, it seems likely that Michel Lambert took Lully under his tutelage when the boy arrived in France. There are several factors which support this assumption, not least of which is the rapidity with which Lully rose in position of the King's court after he left the service of Mademoiselle de Montpensier. In her *Mémoires*, she says:

> *Après avoir été quelques années à moi, je fus exilée; il ne voulut pas me suivre à la campagne; il me demanda son congé; je le lui donnai, et dupuis il a fait fortune, car c'est un grand baladin.*[12]

This took place in October of 1652. On February 23, 1653, Lully danced five roles in the *Ballet de la Nuit* given for the King in celebration of the defeat of the *Fronde*. On March 16, less than a month later, Lully was named composer of instrumental music for the King to fill the office left vacant by the death of the musician, Lazarini.[13]

At this time, Cardinal Mazarin was still completely in control of the affairs of France. Louis XIV was a boy of twelve, and Anne of Austria, though regent, was known to have consulted her prime minister on all matters. Mazarin had learned to know and love Italian opera while he was in the service of Barberini in Rome and made a consistent effort to introduce Italian music in France. An appointment as important as composer of instrumental music would not have been made without his approval. From this evidence, it may be surmised that in 1652 Lully was already an accomplished composer of instrumental music as well as a fine dancer. Furthermore, at the age of twenty, and having been in France for only six years (and that in the service of an enemy of Mazarin) Lully, himself, could not have possessed the influence to seek such a position.

These events can all be explained through the close ties which Lully had with Michel Lambert. Subsequent events show that Lully was, indeed, a true friend. Lambert had one child, a daughter named

Madeleine, who became Lully's wife. Lully's second daughter was named Gabrielle Hilaire after Lambert's sister-in-law, Hilaire DuPuy. On October 11, 1675, Lully and his wife, Lambert, and Hilaire DuPuy, together in three equal parts, bought a house, garden, church-pew, and furnishings together with *des droits seigneuriaux* though Lully later bought out Hilaire DuPuy.[14] Michel Lambert helped to train the singers after the formation of the *Académie*.[15] Besides this, Lully gave Lambert a suite of rooms in the Hôtel de Lully which was built in 1670.[16]

It seems likely, in view of these subsequent events, that Lully was Lambert's student while both were in the service of Mademoiselle de Montpensier. Lully's ability to compose music in the French style, at which Lambert excelled, can be explained in this manner.

The rapidity with which Lully rose to a high position in the King's service can be explained also by Lambert's influence. Knowing the young man's ability (and perhaps thinking of promoting a friendship between him and his daughter who was thirteen years old at that time) Lambert would have been strongly motivated to seek the most rapid advance possible for his protegé. Lambert himself continued to be active in the *ballets de cour* for the King after the *Fronde*, as shown in the lists of performers. Furthermore, the maturity of consecutive thought which seems evident behind Lully's actions would be more logically, if less fantastically, explained if it were supposed that he was following the wise counsel of the older man. What emerges is less the picture of an ambitious wolf, as Lully was depicted by La Fontaine in *Le Florentin* ("and who was the poor defenseless lamb?--certainly not La Fontaine!")[17] than that of a young man whose fortunes were being guided by a solicitous adoptive family.

Later authors writing about Lully have stated that he profited by the disgrace of Mademoiselle to change his colors, joined the triumphant royal party, adroitly seized on the circumstance of Lazarini's death to forward his ambitious plans, and then proceeded to spend the next three years perfecting his art as a composer by taking lessons from three organists, Métru, Gigault, and Roberday. This story of his musical education was based on a court brief printed in 1695 with the title: *Raisons qui prouvent. . .que less Compositeurs de Musique. . .ne peuvent être de la communauté. . .des ménétriers.*[18] The purpose was to show that he was, by instruction, of the French tradition. While Lambert was much sought after as a singer, his compositions were considered to be of minor importance. Métru, Gigault, and Roberday, on the contrary, were highly regarded organists and teachers. While the possibility of Lully's having taken instruction from these men is not excluded, there is the unquestionable fact of longer, more continuous contact between Lully and Lambert in comparison with briefer, less concentrated contact with the three organists--and that at a date when Lully was already assembling his own orchestra and composing music for it. It often happens that a truly gifted composer can gain instruction and experience from a minor artist and, indeed, few "school" composers are as creative as their distinguished masters.

It also is unlikely that Lully changed colors to seize the advantages of being in the royal court because in 1652 the crown was anything but secure. Anne of Austria and Mazarin had been forced twice to flee Paris by revolutions of the parliament and the aristocracy. Louis XIV was King in name only, and there could have been no suspicion that the boy of twelve was to become the most powerful ruler France had known and to have the longest reign of any European monarch. Lully, himself, at twenty, had not settled down to any serious plan of living and, however intelligent he was, it is unlikely that he foresaw the future.

French Citizenship, the Office of *Surintendant*, Marriage, and Collaboration with Molière

Lully's life seems to fall into periods of activity which culminate in major changes in his position in life, followed by years of consolidation through artistic endeavors which represent a new plane of activity. From 1652 to 1661 he participated in court music as a dancer, composer of pieces for the *ballet de cour*, and composer of instrumental music. Gradually, he assumed greater and greater importance as a composer until he became the chief collaborator with Benserade in the production of the *ballets de cour* and by this means placed himself on a different level from that of other composers. This period of activity in his life has been described in Chapter I (pp. 23-26).

The appearance of the *petits violons* in 1656 marks an important step in Lully's career. It is known that he lost no love on the *Vingt quatre violons du roi.* Many sources comment on his opposition to their style of playing, and the anecdote according to which he called them *"maîtres aliborons"* is widely circulated.[19] Italian violinists at that time were not following the same customs as the French in accompanying dances, for while the Italians played more from the written scores, the French regulated the music according to patterns established by the dancers. The accompanying instrumentalists improvised from a skeleton score, ornamenting the bare outlines with profuse divisions until the melody was unrecognizable. The *Vingt quatre violons du roi* were famous for their ability to do this and appeared at all solemn occasions. Lully favored the Italian style in that he wished his music to be played as written. Unable to impose his will as composer on the twenty-four, he formed his own orchestra. The *seize petits violons,* soon augmented in number, played for the King's meals, supplied music for less formal dances, and accompanied the King when he travelled.[20]   As leader of this group, Lully was in the presence of Louis XIV several times each day. Thus, during the years while the young King was forming his musical taste and selecting his associates and advisers, he must also have formed the friendship with Lully which caused him to depend on the composer to supply a steady element of enjoyment and pleasure in his life.

On March 6, 1661, Cardinal Jules Mazarin died, and Louis XIV, at age twenty-three, became King in fact as well as in name. He did not choose a new prime minister, and this on the advice of Mazarin, himself. He described his manner of changing the organization of his government in his instructions to the Dauphin in this way:

> To make completely clear to you the course of my thinking, I believed that it was not in my interest to seek men of more eminent station because . . .it was important that the public should know, from the rank of those whom I chose to serve me, that I had no intention of sharing my power with them. . . that they themselves, conscious of what they were, should conceive no higher aspirations than those which I chose to permit.[21]

Jean-Baptiste Colbert was the instrument Louis XIV chose to execute his decisions. Colbert bought the office of *surintendant* of buildings, became minister of finances when Fouquet was deposed, and gradually became the man through whom the King might be approached. No element of French life escaped the attention of Louis XIV, and every cultural and political institution was given new form.[22]   There is a direct relationship between the assumption of real power by the King and the series of events in Lully's life which took place in 1661 and 1662.

On May 16, 1661, Lully was named *surintendant de musique et compositeur de la musique de chambre*, replacing Cambefort who had died. In December of the same year, Lully became a French citizen by naturalization. On July 3, 1662, he was named *maître de la musique de la famille royale*. On July 24, 1662, he married Madeleine Lambert in the church of Saint Eustache in a ceremony attended by the King and his court.[23]

The marriage certificate is dated July 14 and is signed by Louis XIV, Marie-Thérèse, Anne of Austria, the duc of Rochechouart (father of the future Madame de Montespan), Jean-Baptiste Colbert and his wife, Pierre de Nyert, *premier valet de chambre de Sa Majesté*, and others.[24]   Lambert provided a dowry of 20,000 livres and right of inheritance to his office of composer of chamber music. Louis XIV ratified this hereditary office and united all of Lully's offices in the single office of *surintendant*, the value of which was fixed at 30,000 livres with hereditary rights.

It has never been made clear what was meant by the fixing of the value of the office of *surintendant.* Edmond Radet wrote simply that the value was fixed with hereditary rights. De la Laurencie wrote "fixing at 30,000 livres the sum to be paid by his eventual successor to Lully's inheritors and those of Michel Lambert." Prunières uses De la Laurencie's words only very slightly paraphrased and without quotation marks. However, recent historical studies on the nature of offices in the administration of Louis XIV reveal quite another significance.

When Colbert reorganized taxes, collection of moneys, and commerce, he vastly increased the number of offices which were obtainable by purchase, subject to the approval of the King, while drastically reducing the number of offices which were held by gentlemen who performed no actual services. The men who held such offices paid an annual tax to the King levied as a percentage of the value of the office in order to maintain their positions. Some offices carried with them immediate nobility while others had to remain in a family for a differing number of generations before the nobility became hereditary. Members of the nobility were exempt from paying the *taille,* a tax which was levied either on entire provinces or, in other parts of France, on property. In those parts of France where the *taille* was levied on the entire province, payment was exacted only from commoners and was, therefore, socially degrading.[25] The new system had two important results: first, it allowed Louis XIV to break the power of the nobles who had been responsible for the *Frondes* by placing real power in the hands of men of ability, chosen by him. Second, it opened to men of ability, but of bourgeois birth, the possibility of rising on the social scale. Men were willing to pay sums far in excess of the *taille* in order to demonstrate their membership in the *noblesse de robe.* An office as high as *surintendant* usually carried hereditary nobility.

If this is the true explanation of the wedding present given to Lully by Louis XIV, then two conclusions appear to follow: first, that although the office of *surintendant* was given as a present, Louis XIV nevertheless expected to receive money from Lully in the way of a yearly percentage of that office. This means that in 1661 Lully already possessed a fortune large enough to draw the acquisitive eye of Louis XIV and that of his finance minister. Secondly, while Lully claimed noble origin in Florence, as *surintendant,* and a naturalized French citizen, he acquired French nobility at this time. Certainly, he always signed his name DE LULLY, and his sons, Jean-Baptiste and Louis, both of whom inherited the office of *surintendent,* also used the particule of nobility, as did his third son, the Abbé Jean Louis de Lully. Questions of etiquette were precisely defined in the court of Louis XIV, and it would be hard to believe that his claim of nobility, and the respect and manners accorded to persons of rank, would have been allowed to pass had he not some real rights of this sort. In support of the supposition that Lully was treated on a different plane from other artists is the fact that while Colbert's records show sums of money paid to Molière, Corneille, Quinault, Lambert, LeBrun, Gittard, and a great number of artists, no such sums are recorded as ever having been paid to Lully.[26] It is, however, recorded that in 1726, Destouches paid Lalande's daughter 10,000 livres as purchase price of the "survival" of the *surintendance* of the King's chamber music. Close examination of accounts might permit clarification of this matter.

During the ten years following his marriage and naturalization, Lully again consolidated his position and launched himself into composition of a new musical form. Six children were born, Catherine Madeleine, 1663; Louis, 1664; Jean-Baptiste, 1665; Gabrielle Hilaire, 1666; Jean-Louis, 1667; and Louise Marie, 1668. Louis de Lully was the godson of Louis XIV and Marie-Thérèse, but his baptism was delayed for fourteen years until a suitable date could be found. It should be kept in mind that when Louis XIV became godfather of a child, he did not give a gift, but instead received one from the parents whom he so honored.

During the years 1662 to 1672 Lully not only continued his collaboration with Benserade, but also these are the years of his participation with Molière in the creation of the *comédie-ballet*. These works and the relationship between the two men have already been treated in some detail.[27]

Lully began acquiring property in 1671. On May 28, he bought land on the Rue Sainte-Anne, and on June 13, he purchased another lot on the corner of the Rue Sainte-Anne, and the Rue des Petits-Champs from Messire Prosper Bauyn, conseiller du roi. On July 25, he entered into a contract with the architect, Jean-Baptiste Predo, for 45,000 livres to build the Hôtel de Lully on the latter piece of property and a rental building on the other. Daniel Gittard designed the facade for the Hôtel de Lully, and the interior was decorated in a style typical of the century with gilded rooms, halls of mirrors, and imposing crystal chandeliers. Running short of money, Lully borrowed 11,000 livres from Molière which was to be paid in payments of 500 livres per year drawn from the rental property. The whole sum was paid to Molière's widow after the playwright's death in 1673.[28] This building is still standing and has been restored with a section reserved as a museum.

Lettre Patente, the Foundation of the Académie Royale, and the Tragédies Lyriques

During this same decade, a number of composers were producing pastorales in imitation of the Italian styles. Contrary to the impression usually given in histories of the foundation of French opera, Pierre Perrin was not the first French composer to produce such a work, but he was the first to patent an *Académie*.[29]

Lully's acquisition of the *lettre patente* for the formation of the Royal Academy and Opera is thoroughly documented because the registration of the patent was contested. Not only are the pertinent documents all to be found in the National Archives or in those of the Opera, but also they have been printed in considerable detail in various works in French on the origins of French opera.[30] In spite of this, there still are modern sources containing accounts of this matter based on the invective of Henri Guichard, Sourdéac and Champeron and others who, to further their own fortunes, sought to block the registration of the new *lettre patente*. In view of the significance of the event, and its repercussions on the rest of Lully's life, the facts will be reviewed briefly.

Pierre Perrin, who held the first patent for an *Académie de Musique et de Poésie*, was himself a minor poet who, at the age of twenty-three, married a rich widow who was over sixty. Her son, La Barroire, discovered that his mother had given Perrin money to buy an office in the household of the King's uncle, Gaston d'Orléans. La Barroire had his mother declared mentally incompetent, interned her, and had the marriage annulled. Suit was brought against him as a result of the widow's countersignature for the remainder due in payment for the office Perrin had bought but only partially paid for. In retaliation La Barroire brought suit against the poet and had him jailed for debt seven times over a period of twelve years.

During a brief period of freedom in 1669, Perrin obtained the *lettre patente* permitting him to form an Academy of Poetry and Music through his influence with Colbert to whom he had dedicated a number of his works. The document itself resembles the patents of the *traittants* (men who thought of new schemes to raise money for the crown and who were given patents on their ideas for a percentage of what they were able to collect). Perrin's patent states:

> We permit him to take from the public whatever sums he decides in order to cover the great expenses of performance, as well as theatres, machines, settings, costumes, and other necessary things.[31]

Permission is given to hire guards so that no one, even officers of the King's household, can enter without paying. Therefore, the *lettre patente* given to Perrin proves that French opera, from the very beginning, was to be supported by a paying public.

Perrin associated himself with the musician, Cambert, to exploit the patent he had obtained, but he was jailed before he could supervise the opening of his *Académie*. From his cell, he agreed, by word of mouth, to give half the rights of his patent to his thoroughly dishonest partners, Sourdéac and Champeron, while Cambert became a paid conductor rather than an associate. Perrin also agreed to cede rights to exploit the patent to Henri Guichard, and the musician, Sablières. He then agreed to cede the entire patent to La Barroire in order to get out of prison. He also ceded all the rights to Sablières. And there is still another agreement giving the whole patent to Sourdéac and Champeron who were, at that time, sitting at the door of the opera house with their scales weighing the *louis d'or*, which they pocketed without paying actors, actresses, musicians, or Cambert, to say nothing of Perrin. It is possible that Louis XIV expected to receive some kind of percentage--at least, that was current practice with the patents of the *traittants.*

This disorderly state of affairs could not continue. Colbert, who had engineered Perrin's patent, went to Lully and counseled him to go to Perrin in prison and to buy him out.[32] Lully did so and presented a new patent for registration. The wording of the new patent is clearly based on the first, but there are important differences.[33] The first paragraph states that the King has become dissatisfied with the results of the *Académie* given to Perrin for twelve years, and for that reason that patent is revoked. The reasons for giving it to Lully are stated. The name is changed to *Académie Royale.* The terms concerning financial support are the same as those of the first patent. As in the original patent, no other theater shall be allowed to perform an entire opera without the express permission of the holder of the patent. Lully is expressly forbidden to use any of the King's musicians for public performances. Finally, the new patent is issued for life with rights of succession according to Lully's choice amongst his children.

The registration of the patent was vigorously opposed by all of the people to whom Perrin had given it, singly or together. Perrin, whose debts were now paid, obtained a pension for life from Lully and at last was free from the constant threat of imprisonment. Sourdéac and Champeron gave up their claim to the patent after a few attempts at salvaging their investment, but Henri Guichard was determined to receive what he conceived to be his due.[34] His court brief against Lully is a denunciation of the latter which starts with allusions to Lully's birth, continues by saying that Lully had always loudly proclaimed that opera was impossible in the French language, and ends by saying that foreigners have received altogether too much power in France. Even though Lully won the court case, the printed words of Guichard have served ever since as a basis for judgment of Lully's character.

Guichard continued his attacks in other ways. Lully countered, and the patent was registered by order of parliament through pressure from the King in 1672.[35] Guichard attempted to register a patent for an *Académie des Spectacles* in 1674.[36] The wording is such that it is obvious the author is either the same for all three or else thoroughly acquainted with the texts of the first two. Lully blocked the registration as being an infringement on his own patent. At the same time, Guichard tried to associate himself with Lully's partner, Charles Vigarani, to produce spectacles with machines. In 1675, Guichard tried, with Mademoiselle de Villedieu, to supplant Quinault as Lully's librettist. In the same year, Marie Aubry, a singer in Lully's *Académie* and Guichard's mistress, told Lully that Guichard was trying to bribe her brother, Sebastien, who was employed at the *Académie*, to assassinate Lully by poison, or, if that failed, by dagger. Lully went to the King, and Guichard was tried and jailed. He appealed the decision, won his freedom, and Lully was made to pay the court costs. Sebastien Aubry remained in jail.[37] The briefs from this case consist of nine long reports and the newspapers of the time contain many commentaries. What was the truth of the matter? Henry Prunières believes that the whole thing was a fabrication of Marie Aubry of whom Guichard was tiring and absolved both Lully and Guichard from blame.

Short quotations from Guichard's briefs, songs, and satirical poems are given by various contemporary authors. When these are compared with later biographies of Lully, it is found that they have been quoted, verbatim, to demonstrate that Lully was hated by his contemporaries because of his ruthless and dictatorial methods of enforcing the terms of his patent. Actually, it would appear that Lully, having bought the patent on Colbert's advice, was literally forced into defending his rights, and that what his enemies held against him was that he defended himself ably. The difficulties surrounding the registration of the patent, however, had their effect on Lully who became extremely sensitive to any action on the part of musicians, poets, or court figures to attempt to influence the *Académie* and opera in any way. Any such efforts were immediately seen by him as threats which he must parry in order to defend his position.

Quite apart from the question of *how* Lully came to acquire the patent for the opera is the question of *why* he desired it. Authors consistently have given as his reason a rapacious desire to steal Perrin's money from him. Even though that myth was proven to be without foundation, authors still cite "money and prestige" as the reasons why Lully wanted the patent. Prunières, de la Laurencie, and Borrel have all followed the lead of LeCerf de la Viéville who wrote well after the opera was established and running successfully. It is only reasonable to inquire what Lully could possibly have seen in the *Académie* of Perrin in the way of a successful financial venture. True, the Parisian public flocked to see the pastorales, but the composer and conductor, Cambert, was not being paid. The dancers, actors, and musicians received nothing. Perrin, himself, was jailed for debt. Nobody knows what Sourdéac and

Champeron were receiving, but it would have been impossible for anyone to determine whether it was economically feasible to produce an opera if all the collaborators, actors, dancers, and servants had to be paid. Lully knew the cost of machines, theaters, and costumes, and he must have had some doubts. He knew the difficulties of Molière in keeping a company solvent, and, though their *comédies-ballets* and machine plays were successful, Lully had not yet developed the *tragédie lyrique*. What could have impelled him, successful and wealthy as he already was, to undertake the new and problematic production of an art genre that had not yet been created? Looking at Perrin's *patente* and its results from the point of view of 1671 rather than twenty years later, it would seem to have been a difficult and unrewarding task, full of risks at best.

Ultimately, the *tragédies lyriques* and the *Académie* were those things which Lully valued most and which he thought were his greatest accomplishments. Evidence of this lies in his defense of his sole right to produce them and by his careful planning for their future in his will. What is their nature? These works have never been fully analyzed and for the most part they are not readily available. Only three *tragédies lyriques* exist in modern score, and even these contain a number of obvious errors. Fortunately, the complete edition of Lully's works has recently been resumed by Broude Brothers so that this gap will perhaps be filled.

After the registration of the patent, Lully immediately set about the work of producing his first opera. The most pressing problem to be solved was the choice of a librettist. Lully entered into a contract with Philippe Quinault according to which the poet would be paid 4,000 livres to supply a libretto annually for the opera. The King, also, was to supplement this with 2,000 livres a year, but Colbert's records show that Louis XIV did not pay the entire sum for a number of years.[38]

The next problem was that of providing a stage, settings, machines, and costumes. In order to share the original expense and ensure the provision of these things, Lully entered into a partnership with the machinist, Carlo Vigarani, each of them contributing 10,000 livres to cover the basic costs. Profits were to be divided into equal parts. There is a letter in Colbert's papers in which the finance minister relayed Lully's request to use the *Salle du Louvre* in which to stage his works. Louis XIV replied that Colbert should tell the *Sieur de Lully* that the *Louvre* was not the proper place for public performances.[39] As a result of this, Lully and Vigarani rented a theater on the Rue Vaugirard, and their first production, *Les Fêtes de l'Amour et de Bacchus*, was presented in November of 1672. This work was not a real opera but rather a series of scenes put together by Quinault from *Le Bourgeois gentilhomme, Les Amants magnifiques, La Pastorale comique, Les Fêtes de Versailles, and Georges Dandin.* Lully explained that the reason why the work was not new was because of his difficulties with the registration of the patent. The King was not present at the first performance due to the death of the Duc d'Anjou.[40]

The first *tragédie lyrique, Cadmus et Hermione*, was presented on April 27, 1673, in the theater on the Rue Vaugirard. The account in the Gazette tells of the presence of the King and his court and of the entire satisfaction of all with the new, French opera.[41] Louis XIV gave form to his praise by giving the large theater of the Palais-Royal to the *Académie* the very next day. This stage was occupied by Molière's troup, still disorganized after their leader's recent death. Further cause for enmity was thus added to the dispute between the actors and the *Académie*, for Lully had obtained, in the previous year, an injunction according to which no more than two singers and six violins might be used in production of theatrical works outside of the opera.[42] Since music was an integral part of the theater, this caused considerable hardship. It is true that this was a way for Lully to protect his right to use his own music, written for the Molière *comédies-ballets*, but at the same time it effectively prevented any other composer from writing elaborate scores for machine plays, *comédies-ballets*, or *pastorales*.

On August 14, 1673, Lully obtained an *Arrêt du Conseil* which liberated the instrumentalists of the *Académie* from all obligations to the *Corporation des joueurs d'instruments*. This organization had been formed in 1321 as the *Corporation des Ménétriers* and is the same group as that which in 1695 was taken to court by the composers who also wished to be free of their restrictions. The King of the Minstrels, or violins, as he was called, ruled over all the musicians in France, levying assessments, dues of initiation, and regulating musical affairs. Louis XIV accorded them new statutes in 1658 and, in spite of their disputes with the *Académie* and the composers and organists, the Corporation continued to exist up to 1789.[43] The meaning of Lully's injunction is not quite clear. Descriptions of his method of work, however, show that he required a large number of rehearsals and it can be surmised that the obligations of the Corporation interfered with the tight schedule of the *Académie*. Later accounts indicate that Lully ran the *Académie* in a highly disciplined manner and occupied himself with every facet of the lives of those who worked for him. It is also possible that the "King of the Minstrels" wished to regulate the choice of personnel in the *Académie*, and Lully, who knew that excellence cannot be obtained without careful choice of material, would not have tolerated that.

The second *tragédie, Alceste*, was presented on January 11, 1674. Madame de Sévigné wrote of the extreme beauty of the new opera after having heard parts of it in rehearsal. However, the public production was met by opposition from a cabal organized by those who were jealous of both Lully and Quinault. A satirical song, "O quelle musique de chien," which appears in the *Recueil Tralage*,[44] caused Lully to rewrite a scene in which the barking of Cerberus had been heard throughout. In another letter to her daughter, written after the public performance, Madame de Sévigné retracted her praise. The King allowed it to be known that he approved of *Alceste*, however, and the opera became the rage of all Paris.[45]

Public performances began regularly at five o'clock on Tuesdays, Fridays, and Sundays, with Thursday being reserved for new works.

> . . .the conductor struck the floor with his long baton and the violins warmed up softly, while conversation in the house stopped and the lights were extinguished. Then it was that the first stroke of the bows of the orchestra was heard. Ah! that "premier coup d'archet" of the orchestra of the opera was famed throughout Europe! People came only to hear it and then went away satisfied. . .[46]

It was possible to buy a season ticket which gave the holder the right to attend any performance and to be seated wherever he wished. Some avid opera-goers came to every performance, and since two operas, or at the most three, were presented each year, they heard the same work as many as twenty or thirty times. Copies of the libretto were sold at the door together with candles, and the audience followed the printed text during the performances. In the balcony, disorder reigned as the common people came to meet in secret and to form new alliances, while in the boxes (which were on stage) the *beau monde* came to be seen and would sometimes, to Lully's chagrin, address themselves to the actresses. He tried to put a stop to the practice by raising the prices of these seats and those of the *coulisses*, but unfortunately the patrons who desired such notoriety were well able to pay.[47]

The cabal which met *Alceste* was primarily against Quinault and arose from jealousy on the part of other poets who wished to induce Lully to use other librettists. Mesdames de Montespan and Thianges tried to force La Fontaine on Lully. The poet wrote a pastorale, *Dafné*, which Lully refused and La Fontaine retaliated by writing *Le Florentin* (mentioned above). Lully was greeted at public places with shouts of "Renounce Quinault or you will die!"[48] Boileau also wanted part of the opera, and in his *Avertissement d'un prologue d'opéra* he recounts that Racine wrote a *tragédie, La Chute de Phaéton*, to which he, himself, wrote the Prologue. This work, also, was rejected by Lully and, to judge from Boileau's works, he neither forgot nor forgave. Guichard and Mademoiselle de Villedieu presented two libretti, *Céphale et Procris*, and *Circé et Ulysse*, which were also refused.[49] Lully remained faithful to his contract with Quinault, and there is little doubt that this was due to his perception of the specific requirements of opera libretti which would best serve his purposes.

Thésée was first produced on January 11, 1675, at Saint-Germain, then the residence of the court which had recently returned from the campaign in Flanders. The years 1676 and 1677 are those in which *Atys* and *Isis* appeared. Both were well received, but according to court gossip Madame de Montespan supposedly saw an unflattering portrait of herself in the detestably jealous character of Junon in *Isis*, and Quinault was banished for this offense. It should be remembered, however, that Louis XIV chose the subjects of the operas and followed the rehearsals closely. Furthermore, even after Quinault's banishment *Isis* continued to be presented in Paris without revision.[50]

Meanwhile, Lully had trouble in the heart of the *Académie*. Young musicians came from all Europe to receive their training and worked with the orchestra and as *secrétaires de remplissage*. One of these secretaries, Lalouette, spread the rumor that he, not Lully, had written the best airs of *Isis* and had to be banished from the *Académie*[51]. As a result of all of the pressures on him, Lully fell ill in 1677 and never fully recovered his health as shown in allusions to illness in the dedications of his *tragédies lyriques*.

Psyché of 1678, a work based on the earlier machine play of that name mentioned above, was written to a libretto by Thomas Corneille, nephew of Pierre Corneille. Though the dialogue is considerably changed from the earlier version, the Italian *plainte* in the first act is the same. This fact makes the supposition that Lully wrote the words all the more probable. *Bellérophon*, first produced on January 31, 1679, at the Palais-Royal, was also written by Thomas Corneille and Fontenelle. Boileau claimed to have written the best scenes for this work, and since, unlike Lalouette, he was not a member of the *Académie*, he could not be banished.   According to LeCerf de la Viéville,[52] Lully rejected many drafts by Corneille and Fontenelle and in the end, called in Quinault as a ghost-writer. It was a triumphant success as shown from the accounts of the *Mercure galant* of January, 1679.   The decorations were so magnificent that they were patented. In October, Quinault was again seen at court, and *Bellérophon* was, at last, given at Saint-Germain for the King on January 3, 1680.

This was the first opera to be printed under Lully's supervision by Christophe Ballard, and thereafter all of the *tragédies lyriques* were printed the year they appeared.   Earlier printings come from the Netherlands and are not to be regarded as reliable sources. The Ballard editions are invaluable for it is possible to form a more accurate conception of the works written before *Bellérophon* by comparison of the manuscripts and pirated editions with similar passages and scenes in the Ballard prints.

Proserpine was first produced for the court on February 5, 1680, and the Paris production the following November was staged by Berain. Lully's contract with Vigarani had expired on August 23, 1679, and thereafter he took no associate but, instead, kept the entire financial operation of the opera and *Académie* in his own hands. In the following years, he hired Vigarani or Berain to design the sets, construct and supervise the machines, and to help with the costuming.[53]

On May 10, 1681, the ballet, *Triomphe d'Amour*, was presented. It contained twenty *grandes entrées*, which were danced by female dancers as well as male. This was the first time ballerinas had appeared on stage in public performance, the female roles having been taken previously by men in travesty. According to the regulations of the dance-loving royalty of France, members of the nobility and royalty had been dancing at the sides of professional dancers for many years and could do so without loss of rank or privilege. Lully transferred this practice to the public theater and the novelty of seeing women dancing female roles was very well received. Thereafter, it became a part of the opera. The youngest ballerina in the *Triomphe d'Amour* was Mademoiselle de Nantes, then eight years old, who thus became the first *petite rate de l'opéra*.

For the King's return from Alsace in the autumn of 1681, Lully again donned the make-up and costume of the Mufti in the revival of *Le Bourgeois gentilhomme*. According to the *Mercure galant* (Lyons edition of December) he played the role with such verve that at one point, he jumped on top of the harpsichord which broke into pieces beneath his weight, and Louis XIV, who did not laugh readily, almost fell off his chair. This performance provided the background for Le Cerf de la Viéville's account of Lully's request for, and acquisition of, the office of *secrétaire du roi et de ses finances*.

There are several documents which show precisely how Lully obtained the office of *secrétaire du roi*, and how that office was sold after his death. He bought the office from the widow of Joseph Clausel for 63,000 livres on December 25, 1681.[54] He gave the usual written pledge to pay his part of the debts contracted by the company of *secrétaires* and was accepted by them four days later.[55] When he died, a little more than five years after this, his widow, Madeleine, sold this office to "Sieur Le Comte" for 71,000 livres.[56] The increase in value of the office was by act of the King, who in this way increased his own yearly income.

LeCerf de la Viéville, of ancient lineage himself, ascribed Lully's wish for the office of *secrétaire du roi* to a desire for bona fide nobility. The story he tells is charming, witty, and gives the picture of Lully as a perfect courtier. It is certain that LeCerf meant to be complimentary and to reveal high aspirations on the part of Lully. However, as shown above, Lully already had hereditary nobility, and this fact was in no way altered by the sale of the office of *secrétaire du roi* at his death because his sons continued to use the title of nobility while his daughters had married into noble houses as well. Why did Lully wish to obtain this particular office?

The principal purpose of the *secrétaires du roi* was to underwrite the King's credit. In the words of Colbert, "I entreat Your Majesty to allow me to say that in war and in peace, Your Majesty has never consulted his finances to determine his expenditures." The *secrétaires*, already the wealthiest men in France, busied themselves at making enough money to keep the crown solvent. They were conservative in outlook and dress, and dealt in real estate, banking, and commerce. Why, indeed, should a musician with a flourishing opera house and *Académie* wish to belong to such a group?

Perhaps the chain of events following the registration of the patent is part of the answer. As *surintendant*, Lully felt secure in his position at court where he produced music, both sacred and secular, according to the wishes of the King. This was not the situation insofar as the *Académie* was concerned, as was mentioned above. Furthermore, the opera may have been in financial difficulties for each work cost a fortune to produce, and the crown supplied no money to the *Académie*-- as is proven both by the absence of records of payment in Colbert's papers, as well as by the indication in the patent itself that it was to be supported by public admission. Prod'homme says, "In Lully's day the question (payment of the musicians of the *Académie*) did not come up because. . .he supplied the needs by his own sole effort."[57] Perhaps Lully's desire to become a member of the company of *secrétaires du roi* stemmed from the knowledge that the *Académie* might someday need a source of assured income to supplement an uncertain gate. Curiously, all of the legal problems which had troubled Lully in the 1670's disappeared when he became a *secrétaire du roi*. If the records of the various financial dealings of the members of the body of *secrétaires* were investigated, it might be possible to determine just what part Lully took in their affairs.

From 1681 to his death in 1687, Lully continued to develop the *tragédie lyrique*. *Atys* and *Proserpine* were again performed in January and February of 1682, while *Persée* was premiered in Paris at the Palais-Royal and later was played at Versailles in July. The duc de Bourgogne was born that summer, and in celebration, Lully gave a free performance of his new opera at the Palais-Royal. The *Mercure galant* describes the triumphal arch through which the guests entered and the magnificent fountain which flowed with wine until midnight.[58]

On October 5, 1682, Lully bought for 6,640 livres a house with a garden on the rue de la Madeleine at Ville l'Evêque from Felix du

Verger. He moved into this house in 1683 and rented the Hôtel de Lully.[59]

Phaéton was produced on January 6, 1683, at Versailles. In his dedicatory letter in the Ballard edition Lully speaks of his humble pride that through the patent of his majesty he has been able to present not just a single opera, but also a flourishing *Académie* where singers, dancers, instrumentalists, and composers are being formed according to his majesty's wishes. Indeed, on these occasions, the whole troupe boarded a train of carriages for the trip to Versailles.

In June of 1683, Pierre Gaultier,[60] a musician and impressario, made a contract with Lully for 2,000 livres a year for the *privilège* of opening an *Académie* and opera in Marseilles. The Lyons opera also was founded in the same way that year. Each of these new organizations was run in the same manner as the opera and *Académie* at Paris, and when similar institutions were opened at Rouen, Bordeaux, Dijon, and eventually at Brussels and the Hague after Lully's death, these theaters also operated in the same manner as did the *Académie Royale* at Paris. As Henry Prunières so justly remarks, Lully's work in this area is certainly as important as his artistic works, for these *Académies* were the institutions on which subsequent Conservatories and Opera Companies were modeled.[61]

Amadis, premiered at Paris, January 18, 1684, was the first *tragédie lyrique* not based on Greek mythology transformed to present a protagonist who was the ideal image of a French seventeenth century gentleman. Magnificent in every way, this opera was much discussed in the salons. In the Ballard edition there is a poem of dedication to the King written by La Fontaine who seems to have forgotten his earlier quarrels with Lully. Louis XIV was in mourning for Marie-Thérèse, however, and could hear only fragments in concert.

Roland appeared on January 8, 1685, at Versailles, in the *Grande Ecurie*. Again, La Fontaine wrote a dedicatory epistle. The work was a great success and opened in Paris in March. *Amadis* was also being played, as an article in the *Mercure galant* of June states that on seeing the production the ambassadors from Moscow believed that there was an enchantment of some kind, as such miracles could be the result only of magic.[62]

Lully's daughter, Catherine-Madeleine, married Nicolas de Francine, *maître d'hôtel du roi*, on April 12, 1682. The contract was signed by the king. Lully gave his daughter a dowry of 55,000 livres, and the marriage was lavishly celebrated in the presence of the King and his court.[63] Francine became an employee of the *Académie* and continued to work there after Lully's death.

In 1685, Lully had his oldest son, Louis, interned in the Maison des religieux de la Charité at Charenton. Precisely what the cause was is not known for the terms used are uninformative--deplorable conduct, ne'er-do-well, troublesome child.[64] This was the godson of Louis XIV who interceded on the boy's behalf.

Armide was produced for the first time on February 15, 1686, at Paris rather than at Versailles. In spite of the absence of a royal performance, it was a great success. It has been said that Madame de Maintenon opposed both Lully and the opera, and it was for this reason that operas were no longer performed at court before being seen in Paris after she became the wife of Louis XIV. This is hardly likely for she had been very active in the development of the salon of Scarron before the poet's death, and the serious nature of the *tragédie lyrique* with its presentation of the aristocratic ideal was in sympathy with her own views. Furthermore, *Armide* was the only *tragédie lyrique* written by Lully after Madame de Maintenon married Louis XIV. Henry Prunières surmised that the real reason why *Armide* was premiered in Paris was that there was not enough money for a Versailles performance due to the production of Lalande's *Ballet de la Jeunesse* there that spring. This seems more likely, for the ballet celebrated youth and carefree love, while the opera is concerned with virtue. Of the two works there is little doubt that *Armide* was the more morally edifying. This was the last work on which Lully and Quinault collaborated, and it is also the last *tragédie lyrique* written by Lully. Quinault gave up writing for the theater and undertook the poem, "Extinction de l'hérésie," in 1686. Lully chose the poet, Jean Gilbert de Campistron, to write the libretto for his last complete work.[65]

Acis et Galathée, a pastorale, was first produced at the castle of Anet for the duc de Vendôme and the Dauphin on September 6, 1686. Lully took his whole *Académie* with him by carriage as he did for performances at Versailles. The duke was so pleased that he gave Campistron 100 louis d'or, and to Lully, he gave a precious ring.

Lully's Death

Louis XIV fell ill from an anal fistula in the late fall of 1686 and submitted to a painful operation. Once his recovery was certain, celebrations were given all over France. Lully gave a performance of his *Te Deum* on January 6, 1687, at the church of *Les Feuillants de la rue Saint-Honoré*. He conducted the work personally and inadvertently struck his foot with the long heavy baton. At first, the wound was not very serious but gangrene developed. Doctors advised him to have an amputation but he refused. The duc de Vendôme paid a charlatan, the Marquis de Cavette, 2,000 pistoles to cure the wound, and this expedient failed. Lully had waited too long, an operation had become impossible, and when it became certain that he would soon die he called in his notary, Simon Moufle, and arranged his affairs. He was to be buried in the church of the *Augustins déchaussés* (Petits-pères), and a Mass was to be sung for him in perpetuity. He gave sums of money to *les Filles catholiques de la rue Sainte-Anne* (location of the Hôtel de Lully), the parish poor, the servants of the opera, and to his own personal servants. No one was forgotten. He left the *privilège (Académie)* to Jean-Baptiste (his second son), Madeleine, l'abbé de Lully (his third son), and to his three daughters, but he took care to name his wife as administrator. In that task she was to be aided by his secretaries, Frichet and Colasse, the latter of whom was guaranteed a lifetime pension and dwelling at the Académie. Madeleine was also named executrice of his will. Five days later, Lully was prevailed upon to reinstate his oldest son, Louis, in his inheritance.[66]

Lully died on March 22, 1687, and his funeral was held at the Madeleine with greatest pomp. Michel Cotton constructed a tomb for Lully in the chapel of Saint Jean-Baptiste in the Petits-pères. The bust of Lully by Antoine Coyzevox was flanked by two statues of women representing *la musique légère* and *la musique dramatique.* This tomb was destroyed in the French Revolution, but engravings have been preserved.[67]

As stated above, his widow sold his office of *secrétaire du roi* on April 3, 1687, and in the days that followed, an inventory of his goods was made.

Dans l'écurie
deux cheveaux de carosse hors d'âge
un autre cheval sous poil noir
argenterie, 16,707 livres
pierres et diamants, 13,000 livres
58 sacs de louis d'or, doublons d'espagne, etc.
    250,000 livres
trois maisons, 120,000 livres
Hôtel de Lully, 70,000 livres
Maison rue de la Madeleine, 60,000 livres
Maisons à Puteaux et Sèvres, 50,000 livres[68]

In addition to this, his personal belongings and furnishings were appraised, and amongst his goods were counted the costumes, settings, and machines of the opera and the *Académie de musique.* Altogether, his worth was estimated at 2,500,000 livres.[69]

His second son, Jean-Baptiste, paid the inheritance of the office of *surintendant,* but he died in 1688 without issue. Louis de Lully held the office until his death in 1736. Jean-Louis de Lully, the abbé, had been given the abbeys of Saint Hilaire de Carcasonne, Saint Georges-sur-

Loire, and the priory Saint-Médard de Vitry-aux-Loges. He was the confessor of the duc d'Orléans, and his name also appears on the list of composers working for the *Académie*. Madeleine, his widow, kept the Hôtel de Lully until her death in 1720 when it was sold and the price divided amongst her grandchildren.

Lully left more than wealth to his family. The social status of musicians as a whole remained unchanged in France after his death, but the descendants of the Florentine orphan who had left his country at the age of fourteen bore such names as: La Rochefoucauld d'Etissac, Greffuhle, des Cars, Voguë, Caraman, and Kergolay. It is certain that he held his family in high esteem, for he so encumbered the *Académie* with pensions for all of them that this expense was one of the reasons why the opera had to obtain governmental subsidy after his death.

His greatest legacy, however, was the *tragédie lyrique*. As can be seen in Appendix I, the operas were performed throughout the eighteenth century, the last public presentations being those of *Roland* in 1755, *Amadis*, 1759, *Armide*, 1764, and this same work with revisions by Francoeur in 1781, a scant eight years before the French Revolution began. The style which he set in these works was sufficiently strong so that French opera, alone of all the national operas, maintained a form independent of that of Italian opera. Their influence was great throughout Northern Europe, especially in England, for Purcell's teacher, Pelham Humfrey, was a student of the *Académie* as English royalty was eager to copy French style. In Sweden, Lully's operas were produced in the theater built for the Queen in Drottningholm in 1754--an annex to the Summer Palace which is one of the most beautiful imitations of Versailles. His German students, Georg Muffat and J.F.K. Fisher, carried his training in composition and performance back to their own country where it touched Telemann and Reinhardt Keiser.[70] His influence on the structure and management of the *Académie* has already been treated above.

What was Lully's nature as a man? Existing documents are rare; he left no letters, no explanations, no diaries, and even the accounts of the *Académie* during his administration have disappeared. It seems likely that during the three months of his last illness, he carefully sorted his documents and destroyed anything that might bear personal witness. However, a man is perhaps best known by what he chooses to do or not to do in that area which he considers to be most important in his life. For Lully, the *tragédie lyrique* and the *Académie* were his most important work, and it is through the understanding of the choices he made to give them life that one must seek understanding of the man.

NOTES

[1] Henry Prunières, "Notes musicologiques sur un autographe de Lully," *Revue Musicale*, IV (1928), 47-51.

[2] By Jean Laurent Seigneur de Freneuse, LeCerf de la Viéville, *Comparaison de la musique italienne et de la musique française* (Brussels: F. Foppens, 1704-1706) reprinted in part as "Vie de Lully," *Revue musicale*, VIII (January, 1925), 107-22.

[3] Henry Prunières, "Recherches sur les années de jeunesse de J. B. Lully," *Rivista musicale italiana*, XVII (1910), 646.

[4] Henry Prunières, "Lully, fils de meunier," *Mercure musicale*, VIII (June, 1912), 60.

[5] Jules Ecorcheville, "Lully gentilhomme et sa descendance," *Mercure musicale*, VII (May, 1911), 2.

[6] Prunières, *Lully* (Paris: H. Laurens, 1909), p. 19.

[7] Mademoiselle de Montpensier, *Mémoires* (Paris: Editions Cheruel), V. III, p. 348.

[8] Prunières, "Recherches sur les années de jeunesse," pp. 648-49.

[9] Ecorcheville, op. cit., footnotes on page 6 give the sources as Arch. Nat. Zla 523.

[10] Lionel de la Laurencie, *Lully* (Paris: F. Alcan, 1911), p. 7.

[11] Ibid.

[12] Montpensier, op. cit., Vol. III, p. 348.

[13] la Laurencie, *Lully*, p. 9.

[14] Edmond Radet, *Lully, homme d'affaires, propriétaire et musicien* (Paris: L. Allison, 1891), p. 42.

[15] André Tessier, "Les Répétitions du Triomphe d'Amour," *Revue musicale*, VIII (February, 1925), 123-131. In describing the persons present, Tessier says, "Lambert, who directed the studies of songs in all the operas...."

[16] Radet, op. cit., p. 45.

[17] Romain Rolland, quoted by Prunières in *Lully*, p. 39.

[18] Prunières, ed., *Oeuvres Complètes de J.-B. de Lully*, Les Ballets, Vol. I (Paris: Editions de la Revue musicale, 1931), xiii, n. 2.

[19] Prunières, *Oeuvres Complètes*, Les Ballets, Vol. 1, xx.

[20] Ibid.

[21] Franklin L. Ford, *Robe and Sword* (New York: Harper & Row, 1965), p. 7. (Originally published in 1953 by Harvard University Press.)

[22] For more information on this, see Ford, op. cit., pp. 3-21.

[23]Prunières, *Lully,* p. 19.

[24]Ecorcheville, "Lully gentilhomme," 8.

[25]This matter is still not perfectly clear. For more details, see Ford, op. cit., pp. 17, 27-28, 39, 60, 63, 196, and *passim.*

[26]Pierre Clément, *Lettres, Instructions et mémoires de Colbert* (Paris: Imprimerie Impériale, 1868).   Lists of payments are to be found in volumes V and VI.

[27]See chap. I, pp. 29-34.

[28]Radet, op. cit., p. 50.

[29]Prunières, "L'Académie royale de musique et de danse," *Revue musicale,* VIII (January, 1925), 4.

[30]Nuitter Charles Louis Truinet, and Thoinan A. E. Roquet, *Les Origines de l'opéra français* (Paris: Librairie Plon, 1886). This is the most complete source and is fully documented.

[31]Clément, op. cit., gives the text of the *lettre patente.* It is reprinted in Norman Demuth, *French Opera* (Sussex: The Artemis Press, 1963), Appendix Twenty-three, pp. 268-69.

[32]This is substantiated in a letter from Lully to Colbert in which Lully states that he has acted only as he was counseled by Colbert.   The letter, dated June 3, 1672, is in *Revue des documents historiques: Suite de pièces curieuses et inédites,* ed. Charavay (Paris: 1875), II, p. 112.   It is quoted in many sources, most recently in Robert M. Isherwood, *Music in the Service of the King* (Ithaca: Cornell University Press, 1973), p. 181.

[33]For the complete text, see Appendix II.

[34]Nuitter and Thoinan discuss the affair at length showing Guichard's bias.

[35]Clément, op. cit., pp. 322-23.

[36]Ibid., p. 551.   Also printed in Demuth, op. cit., p. 287.

[37]Nuitter and Thoinan, op. cit., pp. 324-29.

[38]Clément, op. cit., Vol. V, pp. 481-96, shows that before the opera, Quinault received a pension of only 800 livres from the King. He received 1,200 in 1673 and 1,500 a year from 1674 to 1682.   (Colbert died in 1683.)

[39]Ibid., Vol. VI, p. 297.

[40]la Laurencie, *Lully,* p. 37.

[41]Ibid., p. 38.

[42]Clément, op. cit., Vol. V, p. 547.

[43]Jacques Gabriel Prod'homme, "The Economic Status of Musicians in France until the French Revolution." *The Musical Quarterly,* XVI (1930), 86-87.

[44]The words to the song are printed in Isherwood, op. cit., p. 214, and the original source given is Arsenal ms. 6542, no. 172, fol. 259.

[45]Prunières, *Oeuvres Complètes*, Les Opéras, Vol. II, pp. viii-ix.

[46]Prunières, "L'Académie royale," p. 21.

[47]Ibid., pp. 21-23.

[48]Prunières, *Oeuvres Complètes*, Les Opéras, Vol. II, p. x.

[49]Nuitter and Thoinan, op. cit., pp. 321-22.

[50]la Laurencie, *Lully*, p. 51.

[51]Arthur Pougin, "L'Orchestre de Lully," *Le Ménestrel* (February 23, 1896), 59.

[52]Quoted by de la Laurencie, *Lully*, pp. 53-54.

[53]André Tessier, "Berain, créateur du pays d'opéra," *Revue musicale*, VIII (January, 1925), 60-73.

[54]la Laurencie, *Lully*, p. 56.

[55]Ibid.

[56]Radet, op. cit., p. 35.

[57]Prod'homme, "The Economic Status," p. 97.

[58]la Laurencie, Lully, p. 62; cited in *Mercure galant*, August, 1682, p. 120.

[59]Radet, op. cit., pp. 41-42.

[60]Pierre Gaultier of Marseilles was an organist and harpsichordist. He wrote two operas for his *Académie*, but the venture failed within a few years, according to some because of the weighty payments he had to make to Lully. Considering the cost of a single opera, however, 2,000 livres a year is a very small sum.

[61]Prunières, "L'Académie royale," p. 25.

[62]*Mercure galant* (June, 1685), p. 313.

[63]Radet, op. cit., p. 71.

[64]la Laurencie, *Lully*, p. 69.

[65]His last work was the *tragédie lyrique, Achilles et Polyxène*, of which only the first act had been completed at his death. It was finished by Pascal Colasse but never achieved the success of Lully's other works.

[66]la Laurencie, *Lully*, p. 75.

[67]Radet, op. cit., p. 62. See also the engravings in this work. There is a study on the monument, M. E. de Sainte-Beuve, "Le Tombeau de Lully," *Gazette des beaux-arts*, Periode 5, XIV (1926), 198-208.

[68]Ibid., p. 44.

[69]Jean Cordey, "Lully d'après l'inventaire de ses biens," *Revue de musicologie*, XXXVII (July, 1935), 78-83.

[70]For more, see Bernard Champigneulle, "L'Influence de Lully hors de France," *Revue musicale*, XXII (February-March, 1946), 26-35.

CHAPTER III

LITERARY ELEMENTS AND TEXT AS DETERMINANTS OF STRUCTURE IN THE *TRAGEDIE LYRIQUE*

The libretto of an opera determines in large part the entire work. One of the most important differences between Italian and French opera is the emphasis given to the libretto by the French. Lully's choice of Philippe Quinault as librettist was based on his experience in working with Quinault, and the concept of opera which was realized by the two men answered the demand of the French public for better drama in their musical theater than that afforded by either Italian opera or by the pastorales of Perrin, Guichard, and others.

Philippe Quinault (1635-1688) was a pupil and disciple of Tristan l'Hermite. He had written several successful tragedies, comedies, and a number of less extensive works before he collaborated with Lully. He was much in demand before the *Fronde* at the salon of the Hôtel Rambouillet where he read his poems aloud before Corneille, La Rochefoucauld, Mesdames de la Fayette and de Sévigné, the duchess of Longueville, and Mademoiselle de Montpensier. The literary salons, of which this was the first, were ruled over by *les femmes précieuses* who determined the customs of genteel speech and conduct. Quinault had a mild character, willingly adapted himself to the influence and philosophy of the ladies, and he became one of the authors to whom the term "précieux" is attached. Although "les femmes précieuses" were mercilessly ridiculed by Molière and disdained by Boileau, they nevertheless made a valuable contribution to French civilization.

> It was the crowning charm of French society that the sexual stimulus extended to the mind, that the women were roused to add intelligence to beauty, and that the men were tamed by the women to courteous conduct, good taste, and polished speech; in this regard the century from 1660 to 1760 in France marks the zenith of civilization. In that society intelligent women were numerous beyond any precedent; and if they were also attractive in face or figure, or in the solicitude of kindliness, they became a pervasive, civilizing force. The salons were training men to be sensitive to feminine refinement, and women to be responsive to masculine intellect. In those gatherings the art of conversation was developed to an excellence never known before or since--the art of exchanging ideas without exaggeration or animosity, but with courtesy, tolerance, clarity, vivacity, and grace. Perhaps the art was more nearly perfect under Louis XIV than in the days of Voltaire--not so brilliant and witty, but more substantial and friendly.[1]

Quinault was a "précieux" and therefore the opera took on some of the traits of that movement: its vices, including a certain artificiality, but also its virtues.

Lully called his new works for the French stage *tragédies lyriques*, that is to say a *tragédie* completely set to music. The connection with the French classical tragedy is made clear at the same time as is the contrast with Italian opera and the pastorales of Perrin and Gichard. Each *tragédie lyrique* is a true drama, not merely a vehicle to permit the display of voices in glorious arias. The basic form of the play is the prologue and five acts of the classical tragedy. Each act is divided into a number of scenes depending on changes of characters. Four of the thirteen prologues are directly connected with the plays which follow, while the others are allegories in praise of Louis XIV.

Unity of place is not observed because great use is made of ornate settings and spectacular changes of scenery in the *tragédie lyrique*, as it is in the machine play and the *ballet de cour*. Unity of time is ignored insofar as the entire drama is concerned, but as stated above, each scene with the exception of battles and festivals, takes the same amount of time to perform on stage as a similar action would take in real life. Unity of action is observed more strictly in some of the *tragédies lyriques* than in others. There are no scenes, songs, ballets, or spectacles which do not grow out of the drama itself. Liaisons between scenes are always observed and are underscored by musical continuity for the continuo group plays without break from the beginning to the end of each act. The Alexandrian couplet is used very rarely in contrast to the tragedy, but rather free verse like that of the machine play is the rule. In dialogues, there can be as few as three feet per line, or as many as seventeen or more. There is no fixed rhyme scheme except in passages intended to be set as songs in fixed forms.

According to LeCerf de la Viéville[2] and to the prefatory letters by Lully, Louis XIV chose the subjects of the *tragédies lyriques*. Quinault prepared outlines of several stories and presented them to the King who then made his choice. The first ten in chronological order are based on stories from Greek and Roman mythology, while the last three were intended by the King to be about French heroes from the days of chivalry. Ironically, *Amadis de Gaule* was actually from Pays de Gaule, that is Wales, though Quinault, Lully, and Louis XIV believed Amadis to be an authentic French hero.[3] *Roland* is taken from Ariosto's *Orlando furioso* and *Armide* from Tasso's *Jerusalem Delivered*. The intent of the three men, however, was to turn to the history of France and to the portrayal of heroes who exemplified the best and most noble traits of French national character. LeCerf recounts that after the subject was chosen, Quinault and Lully put together a general plan after which Quinault wrote the whole play. The text was then presented to the

King Choose subj, Quinault + Lully made a general plan, - Quinault
wrote plays, Academie corrected + revised it, Lully began
composition.

French *Académie,* of which Quinault was a member, who corrected and revised it. Lully began his composition only at this point, but according to LeCerf, the composer demanded hundreds of revisions in spite of the approval of the *Académie.* These changes were not always merely to facilitate musical setting. For example, Lully objected violently to the character of Phaéton and required Quinault to make his protagonist less subject to ambition.

Quinault did not merely dramatize the myths and tales of chivalry. The actual subject material was used as a pretext for the presentation of two basic themes: glory and love. These themes are presented in each play, and what emerges is an idealistic concept of the manner in which the individual of noble character should conduct his or her life. The protagonist who lives according to this ideal is rewarded for his acts by going from a state of unhappiness to one of bliss, by being united in perfect love with a woman of noble and constant character, while the protagonist whose acts are unworthy of the ideal is punished and his downfall is brought about. An important distinction is made here between the Greek and French attitudes towards the agency by which the denouement is accomplished. In the *tragédie lyrique* both triumph and downfall are accomplished by supernatural means. In view of the importance of these themes, *la gloire* and *l'amour* must be defined as they· are presented in the *tragédie lyrique.*

The real meaning of *la gloire* is the honorable reputation acquired through the magnanimous performance of great deeds by a man of high rank; a prince, a legendary hero or a god. The specific deeds performed are of less importance than the motivation of the protagonist. The hero must be motivated by a gratuitous desire to help those less able than himself; he rescues maidens in distress, he frees entire nations from the menace of terrifying monsters, and he breaks the power of enchanters over their prisoners. His reward is never the direct result of any particular act of heroism but rather is brought about by the intervention of some supernatural power. Furthermore, he must doubt his ability and feel that he has forever lost his beloved. Putting aside his personal unhappiness, he acts to protect others or to secure their happiness, risking his life to do so. Therefore, while he is rewarded by attaining union in perfect love, love is not his motivation. He is motivated by the desire to live in accordance with a standard of conduct which demands uprightness of character as an end in itself without thought of reward. Paradoxically, because the ultimate reward is union in perfect love, ideal love represents the greatest good.

In the *tragédie lyrique* ideal love is presented in sharp contrast to passion. Ideal love strengthens the hero in his desire to perform great acts of courage, while passion can cause a hero or heroine to abandon all honor, pride or glory, and will lead to his or her downfall. Ideal love is constant and true, and the lover must be faithful in heart regardless of obstacles in his path. As conceived by a noble soul, love is not always fulfilled since no one can command love. The lady's consent is necessary, and if it cannot be won, then glory demands that the hero be master of his emotions and renounce his love. Jealousy exists in even ideal love, but the desire for the happiness of the person loved is always stronger, whereas in passion, jealousy provokes hatred and the desire for vengeance. Ideal love is the ultimate good of which only the noblest souls are capable, while passion is condemned because it is incompatible with honor and glory.

Paul Bénichou has described the manner in which concepts of ethics in the seventeenth century influenced the writing of Pierre Corneille, "*les précieux*," Racine, and Molière.[4] The ideals of glory and love as presented in the *tragédie lyrique* are very similar to the ideals portrayed in the Corneillian *tragédies*. Bénichou traces the origins of these ideals as follows:

> In this respect Corneille and his contemporaries were echoing a tradition of fairly distant origin. At first glance it may seem anachronistic to apply the term *feudal* to Corneille's inspiration. But there is no other word to designate what persists in the psychology of the well-born gentleman of the seventeenth century, of the old ideas of heroism and bravado, magnanimity, devotion to duty, and ideal love, all opposed to the aristocracy's more modern tendencies toward simple moral elegance or *honnêteté*. The ideas, sentiments, and the behavior that formed a part of feudal life were still alive long after the decline of feudalism. --- There exists an uninterrupted current of thought which the Renaissance modified, and in a sense, reinforced, rather than reversed. The prestige of heroic chivalry was revived when contact was established once more with the rediscovered heroes of antiquity, as seen through the eyes of Plutarch and Seneca. Similarly, the ideal of love inherited from the Middle Ages drew new strength from the rediscovery of Plato.[5]

The ideals of love and glory permeate the literature of the early seventeenth century and were extremely popular both within the royal circle and with the old aristocracy. While Louis XIV suppressed the freedom of the nobles and lessened their importance after the *Fronde*, he nevertheless embraced the aristocratic ideal of conduct as being that by which a great prince should govern himself, and the new nobles of bourgeois origin were happy to bask in his reflected glory. The old aristocracy, on the other hand, bitterly resented the suppression of their former independence and found pleasure in identifying themselves with the heroes and heroines of Lully who exemplified the feudal and chivalric tradition. Both factions flocked to see the *tragédies lyriques* and attended performances of the same work repeatedly. Works which are able to draw such audiences must reflect the prevalent social philosophy so that identification with what is taking place on stage is established.

Each of the *tragédies lyriques* is based on a story which was already known to the audience; therefore, they did not attend to learn the outcome but rather to experience the manner in which that outcome was brought about. Whereas in Greek tragedy a change of state in the life of the protagonist occurs as the result of a flaw in character, in the *tragédie lyrique* the change of state is determined by whether or not the protagonist is true to the ideals of love and chivalry. The works are infused with these ideals. The allegorical prologues present them at the outset, the drama itself is based on them, and in addition to this Quinault frequently interjects short commentaries in which they are again set forth. An analysis of *Cadmus et Hermione* shows how the poet proceeded. The French names of mythological persons are used when referring to characters in the *tragédies lyriques*, while English equivalents are used in describing the myths.

Cadmus et Hermione

The prologue of *Cadmus et Hermione* is based on the eighth fable of the first book of Ovid's *Metamorphoses*. Python is evoked from the matter left after the great flood by the power of Envie. He becomes a monster so strong and furious that only Apollon himself is great enough to rid the earth of this scourge, after which the god calls on the inhabitants of earth not to celebrate his greatness but rather to enjoy their own happiness. Similarity in theme connects the prologue and the opera.

In the myth of Cadmus, which was told in part or in whole by many authors, the hero is the brother of Europa. He consulted the oracle at Delphi and was told by Apollo to forget his search and to found his own city. He would meet a heifer, and he must follow her to the place where she would lie down to rest, and there he must build. This was the manner in which Thebes was founded. However, there was a dragon who guarded a near-by spring, and one by one this monster slew all of Cadmus' companions. He fought the creature, and when he killed it, Athena appeared to him and told him to sow the dragon's teeth in the earth. Armed men sprang up from the furrows and, turning upon each other, they fought until all but five were killed. These Cadmus persuaded to help him build Thebes. However, he first had to serve eight years of bondage to Ares to expiate the murder of the serpent. Athena then arranged his marriage with Harmonia, daughter of Aphrodite and Ares.

A number of changes have been made in the myth, but the most important one would appear to be an error. Hermione speaks in the opera of being the daughter of Aphrodite and Ares, but Hermione was the daughter of Menelaus and Helen of Troy. The names Harmonia and Hermione were inadvertently mixed up. Other changes stem from dramatic necessity and custom.

Hermione has been captured by the giant Draco who wishes to marry her against her will. Cadmus is determined to free her, though he may die in the attempt. Pallas reassures him with these words:

> Qui peut-être contre l'Amour quand il s'accorde avec la Gloire?[6]
>
> Who can be against Love when it is in accord with Glory?

To reach the palace where Hermione is held captive, Cadmus must slay the dragon. The comic character, Arbas, is the servant of Cadmus and demonstrates the nobility of his master through contrast. Arbas flees in terror as the dragon approaches, but when Cadmus leaves to search for Hermione, Arbas claims that it was he who slew it. In his protestations of love to Charité, Arbas' flippancy contrasts with the steadfast feelings of his master, while the jealousy of the nurse of Hermione is portrayed in such a way as to make that emotion seem quite ridiculous. These two characters are outgrowths of the long line of theatrical ancestors going back at least to the Roman comedies.

Hermione tries to convince Cadmus that he must forget her in noble renunciation of love since not to do so will imperil his life. He is adamant in his resolution, fights successfully, sows the dragon's teeth, and gains an army with which to combat the Géant. Unable to win the fight fairly, the Géant makes three more giants appear through magic. Pallas intervenes saying:

> Protéger la vertu d'un Prince magnanime,
> C'est le plus doux employ des Dieux.[7]
>
> Protecting the virtue of a magnanimous
> Prince is the sweetest employment of the gods.

Junon, who was protecting the Géant, carries Hermione away on a rainbow just as the lovers are about to be united. Cadmus is mourning his loss when Pallas appears to tell him that Jupiter has judged in his favor, and the mortals are transported to Parnassus to celebrate their marriage.

The themes of love and glory are presented in three ways: through the story itself, through comments revealing the characters of the hero and heroine, and through contrast with characters of lesser stature. Cadmus and Hermione are shown to be noble souls and are rewarded by being united in marriage, while Junon's intervention serves to make clear that their reward is not for anything they have done but rather for what they are. The magnanimous quality of the heroes of the play and prologue is shown by Apollon's comment that the people should celebrate their joy and by Pallas' statement quoted above.

In all of the *tragédies lyriques* which followed *Cadmus et Hermione*, Quinault proceeded in much the same manner, altering the subject material so that love and glory are portrayed. The differing ways in which this was done will be described briefly for each opera with a more detailed study given in Appendix III.

Alceste

The story of Alceste has undergone considerable transformation. Quinault's Alceste is not a brave mother sacrificing herself for the good of her children, but rather a bride on the day of her marriage. She is loved not only by Admète, but also by Alcide and Lycomèdes, King of Scyros. Her servant, the nymph Céphise, is also loved by more than one man, and her inconstancy contrasts amusingly with Alceste's fidelity and depth. Lycomèdes organizes a festival to celebrate the coming marriage and uses it as a pretext to kidnap Alceste and carry her off to Scyros. Admète and Alcide go to her rescue. In the ensuing battle Admète is fatally wounded, and Alceste, seeing that no one will sacrifice themself for him, saves him at the last moment by taking her own life with a dagger. Alcide volunteers to go to the underworld to bring back Alceste on the condition that he, not Admète, will become her husband. Alcide succeeds in bringing Alceste back to earth but though the two formerly betrothed lovers are loyally trying to keep their bargain, their eyes betray their true emotions. Alcide is struck by their nobility and constancy and renounces his claim to Alceste.

> Non, non, vous ne devez pas croire
> Qu'un vainqueur des tyrans soit tyran à son tour:
> Sur l'Enfer, sur la mort j'emporte la victoire.
> Il ne manque plus à ma gloire
> Que de triompher de l'amour.[8]

> No, no. You must not believe that a conqueror of tyrans would
>   himself become a tyrant.
> I have vanquished the Underworld and Death.
> The only thing my Glory lacks is conquering Love.

To which the two lovers answer:

> Ah!   Quelle gloire extrême!
> Quel heroïque effort!
> Le vainqueur de la Mort
> Triomphe de lui même.[9]

> Ah, what extreme Glorys!
> What an heroic effort!
> The vanquisher of Death
> Triumphs over himself.

The use of love as a reason for Alcide's heroic act is an example of the type of thing which was ridiculed by those who criticized "les précieux."

> Certes le sujet d'Andromaque (*sic*) ainsi conté prêterai à rire. -- Je doute qu'il ait pris la peine de relire la tragédie d'Euripide que Racine lui reprochait d'avoir travestie.[10]

> Certain, the subject of Adromaque (*sic*) told in this manner is laughable. I doubt that he had taken the trouble to reread the tragedy of Euripides which Racine accused him of having travestied.

Prunières goes on to say that it was the Italian models which inspired Quinault, together with the necessity of placing some great event in each act which caused the poet to transform the story in this manner. However, if the ideals of love and glory are seen as the basic themes of the Lully-Quinault *tragédies lyriques*, then Quinault's transformation expresses another facet of courtly love and aristocratic conduct. Alcide's magnanimity and the noble renunciation of reward for his heroic actions are presented in an even more favorable light than the happiness of Alceste and Admète, showing that if there is conflict between love and honor, then the noble soul will choose honor.

The character of Céphise provides an interesting sidelight. Céphise is flighty, but she is nevertheless present at all of the important acts in the opera. There is, however, no legend or myth referring to this nymph. On the other hand, the river Cephissus ran by the estate of Academus, who revealed to the Spartans the hiding place of Helen of Troy. The estate was later called Academia: a beautiful, well-watered garden, where philosophers met and discoursed.[11] What with the nymphs of the Marne and the Seine, it would seem that through Céphise Quinault and Lully were referring to their own *Académie*, comparing it to that of the ancient Greeks.

Thésée

The character of Thésée, the youth, is an effective one to use in presenting the image of an ideal hero suggesting comparison with the young King of France. The addition of Aeglé to the story and the device of having Médée love Thésée permit Quinault to show the differing facets of jealousy in ideal love and in passion. Aeglé is willing to sacrifice her own joy and happiness to save the life of her beloved, while Médée's jealousy requires the most terrible vengeance. It is noteworthy that once again the reward of the protagonist has not been allowed to result from natural means from his heroism, but rather his happiness comes from Minerve's intervention.

Atys

The transformation of the story of Cybelle and Atys is the most drastic of any of the changes made by Quinault from the original sources. The reason for this can only be subject to speculation. It is well known that Louis XIV was violently opposed to sodomy, and the cult of Cybelle developed a sodomitic priesthood. Many songs, epigrams, and court gossip were concerned with Lully's morals, and, in spite of his wife and family, he was once openly acccused of sodomy. Did the King choose the subject of *Atys* with the intention of subtly warning his *surintendant* to change his ways or beware? If so, it would appear that Lully and Quinault outwitted the King who, at that time in his life, had reason to be particularly susceptible to insinuations that he who places passion above duty and glory will surely be punished. Was it the real criticism of himself in *Atys* rather than the imagined criticism of Mme. de Montespan in *Isis* which caused Louis XIV to banish Quinault from court for two years? It seems likely and, though such speculations are difficult to prove, the humor inherent in the whole situation would not have been lost on the court!

Isis

The story of the myth of Io remains essentially unaltered in the *tragédie lyrique Isis*. Though poorly conceived love is portrayed, and Jupiter is criticized for his lack of mastery of his emotions, the main theme of the work is the excessive jealousy of Junon. The court, as previously mentioned, saw in this play a direct allusion to the jealousy of Madame de Montespan for a younger rival. Whether for *Isis* or for the preceding drama, Louis XIV banished Quinault from court for two years during which time Lully had to make the best of Thomas Corneille and his nephew, Fontenelle, as librettists.

Psyché

The libretto of *Psyché* was the first written by Corneille and Fontenelle, and there is a considerable difference in their manner of treatment and that of Quinault. There are few actual changes in the story, and those are mostly in the interest of tightening the structure. Instead of having Cupid arrange the sacrifice of Psyché, Corneille and Fontenelle make Venus' jealousy the reason why the oracle demands Psyché's exposure. Not until then will Venus cease to send plagues and pestilence to the King's people. Venus also replaces Psyché's sisters as the temptress who inveigles the girl to attempt to see her lover. The tasks given to Psyché are condensed into the single task of seeking Proserpine's vanity box. In all other ways, the story follows the main outlines of that of Apuleius.

The element of magnanimity is lacking as a consistent part of the character of the protagonist, and love is portrayed as being supreme in the universe. The theme of glory is present in Psyché's willingness to sacrifice herself to save her people from the wrath of Venus. Curiosity and lack of trust cause her downfall. Psyché does not redeem herself by any formidable act of courage and self-sacrifice, rather her virtue lies in the constancy and depth of her love, and for this she is rewarded--or is it that Cupid cannot live without her, as he, too, is a victim of his own medicine? Jupiter, also, is subject to love, and Venus must bow her proud head and submit. Therefore, there is considerable contrast between *Psyché* and the *tragédies lyriques* written by Quinault since glory and honor are obedient to love in Psyché.

Bellérophon

The myth of Bellérophon has been considerably scrambled by Corneille and Fontenelle. Bellérophon, the peerless hero who gives himself only to the pursuit of glory, is loved by both Stenobée and Philonoe. Stenobée is the widow of Proteus, and Philonoe is the daughter of the new King. (Thus, Proteus is dead in the *tragédie lyrique*, and Bellérophon does not marry his daughter.) The new King gives Philonoe to Bellérophon for his great deeds. After the magnificient celebration of their engagement, Bellérophon is left alone with Stenobée who tells him that it was she who had him exiled from Argos. Then she feared and hated him, but now she loves him. He refuses to answer her advances so she goes to the magician, Amisodar, and asks him to help her gain vengeance. Amisodar calls for the terrible monster from the underworld, and Stenobée tries to persuade the King that the monster has come because he disobeyed the order to destroy Bellérophon. The King remains loyal to his friend, and with Philonoe, he pleads with

Bellérophon not to expose himself to danger. They consult the oracle of Apollon who tells them that a son of Neptune will calm the monster and marry the princess. Bellérophon refuses to be dissuaded from trying to save the people even though he must lose his beloved and his life. Stenobée, on discovering his resolve, is frightened for him and asks Amisodar to destroy the monster, but he refuses. Bellérophon is aided in battle by Pallas, and after the monster has been vanquished, the goddess announces that the oracle has been fulfilled for Bellérophon is the son of Neptune. Furthermore, as Pallas says:

La valeur et l'Amour font toujours des miracles.[12]

Courage and Love always produce miracles.

In the midst of the celebration which follows the King seeks to know the cause of Stenobée's unhappiness. She reveals her perfidiousness and tells them that she has taken poison and is dying for her love and for her crime. All exclaim:

Quel excès de fureur![13]

What an excess of rage.

The King calls on the entire company to forget their past miseries and rejoice in the future happiness of Bellérophon and Philonoe.

The return to the classic themes of glory and love is obvious, giving added weight to the idea that Quinault was secretly collaborating with Thomas Corneille and Fontenelle. If the character of Stenobée and the reaction to her suicide seem forced, it is because of the difference in concept between ideal love and passion. To the mind of a person imbued with the aristocratic ideal, she is doubly to be blamed; first, because of giving in to a shameful passion to the extent of seeking to destroy the person she loves for jealousy, and secondly because she takes her own life instead of courageously mastering her feelings. Her greatest treason is against her own glory and changes made from the myth tend to bring this out. The restraining influence of the ancient law of hospitality has been replaced by love and friendship in order to be more in keeping with the social concepts of seventeenth-century France. After *Bellérophon* Quinault was allowed to return to court, and the remainder of the libretti for the *tragédies lyriques* of Lully are by him.

Proserpine

The prologue of *Proserpine* is devoted entirely to the portrayal of glory, while the nature of ideal love is treated in the opera itself. The character of Pluton has been modified by the words Quinault has put in his mouth, for Pluton is not nearly as appealing in the myth as he is in the *tragédie lyrique*. Pluton's love is shown in such a sympathetic light, pure and constant, ever faithful, subservient to Proserpine's wishes but never faltering. Supposedly there is no comic element in the later *tragédies lyriques*, but it is decidedly amusing when Pluton states that he sees no reason why that old lecher Jupiter has to interfere with the only love Pluton has ever known!

Persée

In *Persée* events from the myth have been telescoped due to the theatrical necessity of limited time. Andromède's appearance in the first act is in accordance with the rule of French drama that all of the main characters should be introduced in that act. Otherwise, Quinault has interwoven the various details of the story so as to make an increasingly tense succession of events leading to the climax and conclusion. Persée and Andromède represent the ideal hero and heroine. Phinée is the arch-type of a villain, already presented several times in the *tragédies lyriques*, willing to kill for jealousy, full of deceit and trickery.

Mérope, however, represents an entirely new kind of female character, and in one sense she is superior to both Persée and Andromède for she knows that she is not loved and nevertheless acts nobly, helping others to attain a happiness which she, herself, will not be granted. It is possible that the portrayal of her goodness was simply motivated by the desire to present nobility of character which was truly disinterested. On the other hand, there was at this time a woman at court on whom the character of Mérope may have been modeled, i.e., Madame de Maintenon.

Phaéton

Phaéton, like *Atys*, has a tragic ending because the protagonist has transgressed both glory and love. Phaéton abandons his first sweetheart out of ambition to gain personal power, and he brings ruin to the earth in the hope of making a pretentious display of his lineage. He lacks loyalty and constancy in love, and he is punished because his sole motivation is personal gain. He is warned in advance but refuses to consider the suffering he will cause through the realization of his egotistical desires. Even the prediction of his own downfall does not deter him. No other *tragédie lyrique* depicts with such clarity the ideal that the hero must be animated by the magnanimous wish to perform acts of great bravery.

Amadis

Amadis was the first *tragédie lyrique* which was not based on ancient mythology. Louis XIV chose one of the most widely read stories in France to be the subject.

Amadis was thought by Henry Prunières to be the best of the Lully *tragédies lyriques*. When he became aware that he would be unable to complete the modern edition of the works of Lully because of his increasing illness, Prunières abandoned the chronological order and chose to finish his work with *Amadis*.

> Le succès fut immense. Les airs succédaient aux airs avec enchantement. . . .Lully avait oublié les scrupules littéraires qui le retenaient jusque là, et s'était abandoné à la joie de créer de souples mélodies aux lignes expressives, sans s'embarraser de la césure et de la rime.[14]

> It was an enormous success. One air followed another as if by enchantment. Lully forgot the literary scruples which had restrained him and abandoned himself to the joy of creating supple melodies with expressive lines, not bothering with caesura and rhyme.

Lully's dedicatory letter also shows that he considered *Amadis* to be a departure from his previous style since it concerned a hero of France rather than a mythological character.[15]

All France believed that *Amadis de Gaule* was a French hero-- even an ancestor of the royal family.[16] François I read the story of Amadis while he was a captive in Spain. On his return he asked Nicholas de Herberay, Seigneur des Essarts, to make a translation which immediately gained great popularity with the court. The author most commonly associated with *Amadis* is Garci Ordoñez de Montalvo who claimed to have translated the first four books from a Portuguese manuscript written by a certain Vasco Lobeira. A reconstitution exists of the Amadis of Lobeira written in Portuguese in 1926. This was duly translated into French.[17] It appears more likely, however, that Montalvo was claiming the origin of his tale to be a nonexistent manuscript, one of the common practices of the time. The fifth book was found, according to Montalvo, in a deserted, half-destroyed tomb near Constantinople.

Originally Amadis de Gaula, Gaule, Galles, or other variants of spelling, was probably part of the literature which sprang up about the early kings of England. Gaule was taken by the French to mean France. Herberay and those who read him blithely ignored the fact that the preponderance of characters from the first four books come from Great Britain, Ireland, and Scotland as well as Gaule. The action in book one specifically mentions Windisorre, Bristoya, Escoce, Irland, and voyages passing between these places.[18] The terms Gaula, Gaule, and Galles were used indifferently to refer to Wales or those portions of France where the Gaelic tongue was spoken. Eugène Baret presents the idea of Welsh origin for Amadis convincingly,[19] and his evidence is easily checked in the Vaganay reproduction of the first book of *Amadis* as translated by Herberay. How the story passed from England to Portugal or Spain is unknown.

The position which the story soon gained in France was both controversial and widespread. Edouard Bourciez wrote,

> Amadis became the breviary wherein the court of Henri II learned to think and express its sentiments.[20]

Catherine dei Medici used scenes from the book in her court entertainments. Festivals were planned around enchanted towers from which fair maidens were rescued, and then the whole setting would be put to the torch.[21] François de la Noue complained that everyone was "Amadising their speech" and opposed the romance on the grounds that it had a bad effect on young people. Others took the opposite viewpoint maintaining that no better book could be found for teaching young people the proper manner of behaving and expressing themselves.[22]

These two viewpoints remained the poles of the dispute which centered around *les précieux*. Eugène Baret writes that the circle who gathered at the Hôtel Rambouillet and of which Quinault was the chief literary figure, weakened and denatured the spirit of ancient chivalry.

> A des moeurs réelles, historiques, viriles surtout, succéderent des sentiments convenus, chimériques, puériles.[23]

> To true morals, historical, and above all virile, conventional sentiments were substituted--chimerical, puerile.

He goes on to say that it is not that love has an important place in the works of the novelists and playwrights inspired by *les femmes précieuses*, but that the importance and overwhelming pervasiveness given to love is to the detriment of the male virtues which had kept the old romances of chivalry from being sentimental and impossibly fantastic from the point of view of heroism.

> Love becomes an end in itself and ceases to be only the motive.[24]

If these statements, which are echoed by many authors, are examined in light of what *Amadis* actually contained, they prove to be somewhat lacking in logic. When Amadis runs his horse over his defeated victim to make sure the man is dead, and sends such gory souvenirs as Arcalaüs' hand and the head of Arcabonne's husband to his future father-in-law, he is behaving in a manner which was quite acceptable in the days of chivalry but which was considered barbaric in the seventeenth century. By the same token, when Amadis faints away at the mere thought of Oriane, is so affected by the sight of her that he drops his sword in the midst of a tournament, and sheds bitter tears all night thinking of her so that his friends wonder if he is ill, his behavior is much more sentimental than that of any seventeenth-century gallant, for it is entirely lacking in balance.

The plot of *Amadis* is rather disjointed in comparison with many others, and there are two reasons: the medieval romances were constructed of incidents which were not interrelated but instead were woven loosely about a main theme, in this case, the love of Amadis and Oriane. Secondly, Quinault depended very much on the audience's prior knowledge to fill in the gaps in this drama for the story was extremely well known. An example of this is the doubt which Oriane shows of her lover in the first act. She seems quite petulant in the *tragédie lyrique*, but the audience knew that Amadis had rescued Queen Briolanie and thereafter had remained in attendance at her court for several months, which more than justifies Oriane's jealousy!

Since Amadis was a knight who embodied the spirit of chivalry, all of the elements of ideal love and glory are portrayed in the opera, though Quinault has mixed the events and characters freely. Amadis and Oriane are personifications of noble character. This is shown through their actions, through the reflections on their fine qualities by Florestan and Corisande, and through contrast with the characters of Arcabonne and Arcalaus.

Roland

The basic concept underlying Quinault's *Roland* is that badly conceived love will bring ruin even to a noble soul. Angelique is not unworthy of love because she refuses Roland, but rather because she chooses a man who is not worthy of her. Medor is portrayed as being weak enough to attempt suicide if he cannot live near Angelique, and though they marry, it is a clandestine affair followed by immediate flight. Roland receives many signs that Angelique is unworthy of his love, and he goes mad because he refuses to master his own passion. It is noteworthy that there are no songs glorifying youth and the pleasures of carefree love such as appeared in earlier operas. This possibly reflects the fact that Queen Marie-Thérèse died between the performance of *Amadis* and the writing of *Roland.* Madame de Maintenon was now wife of Louis XIV, and her steadying influence had become dominant at court.

Armide

In *Armide* it is shown that magic, or elements of supernatural power, cannot assure the rewards of ideal love. Even Armide, a character of noble stature, could not succeed through dissimulation and is punished by loss of Love.

From the above it can be seen that glory and ideal love are the central themes of all of the *tragédies lyriques* written by Quinault regardless of the actual story. This was not the result of a preoccupation with love, nor was it mere flattery and praise of Louis XIV, but instead the presentation of concepts which would have the wide understanding and appreciation from the audience for which the works were intended. The ideal was not invented by Quinault and Lully, but was the echo of the aristocratic ideal.

The reasons why the *tragédies lyriques* have been described as cold and its characters likened to impersonal statues without human emotions are the same as the reasons given by Bénichou for similar criticism applied to the works of Corneille. There were two opposing trends in French thought and literature in the seventeenth century; that of noble sentiments as depicted in romances and heroic poems and that of reason and nature found in essays, didactic works, and stories. The end of the century saw the triumph of reason and nature and with it, bit by bit, disappeared the understanding and sympathy with the aristocratic ideal. Glory became an empty shell, and love came to be seen only as passion, a force of nature. Heroes who spoke of being masters of themselves were no longer seen as ideal. It is interesting to note that the nature of the cuts made in the Lully operas after his death bears out this reasoning. The Lajarte edition is based on copies used in actual performances of the works over a number of years and progressively more and more of the scenes showing the nature of love and glory were omitted until what remained was a disconnected series of magnificent celebrations and the bare outlines of the plots.

Dramatic Progression and Delineation of Character in the *Tragédie Lyrique*

The strength of the Quinalt librettos lies in the dramatic progression and in the delineation of character. Each act proceeds to a logical conclusion or else builds up to a twist in plot. In either case, the conditions for the next act are set. The manner of construction is slightly different for each play, but the basic outline is that of the French tragedy in which the main characters and action are introduced in the first act, the conflict made plain in the second, in act three matters are brought to a point so that the conflict must be resolved, the next contains the climax, and in the final act the results are made known and conclusions are drawn.

Atys is a good example of this construction. Quinault builds the tension through the order in which he introduces his characters and the manner in which they reveal their feelings. He begins with Atys who is preparing for the arrival of the goddess, Cybelle. Though Atys claims to be happy in the freedom of his heart from love, he reveals his true feelings to his confidant though he does not name his beloved. Sangaride is introduced next and is recognized by the audience as being the object of Atys' affection well before the lovers reveal their hearts to each other. Sangaride also tells her confidant of her love. The tender scene which follows serves to relax the tension momentarily, and by this means the magnificent spectacle of the coming of Cybelle to earth is given an emotional intensity it could not otherwise have had.

The second act is centered around the goddess. Celanus, the king to whom Sangaride is betrothed, would have wished to be chosen as Cybelle's priest, while Atys feigns indifference. Cybelle chooses Atys who is tormented by jealousy when Celanus says he will console himself by marrying the little beauty, Sangaride. Cybelle tells her confidant that she is overwhelmed with love for Atys and has given up her place of honor for him. This scene serves the same dramatic purpose as the love scene in the first act because it is immediately followed by the celebration in honor of Atys. As in the first act a celebration which might be only a joyful occasion is thus filled with tension.

The third act is built around the "slumber" scene. Atys is undecided what to do. On learning that Sangaride wishes to throw herself on Cybelle's mercy to avoid marriage to Celanus, Atys is shocked, but when she appeals directly to him, he loses his resolve to follow honor. In his dreams he sees the consequences of both paths of action open to him, and Cybelle tells him she will fulfill the dream. Sangaride and Atys nevertheless ask the goddess to free Sangaride from her marriage vows. Cybelle tells her confidant that she realizes Atys does not love her but that she wishes to be sure whether or not he actually will betray her and therefore gives orders that all wishes and desires of Atys be fulfilled. Quinault has clarified the issues and brought the drama to the point where a climax has become necessary.

Tension is momentarily relaxed in the beginning of act four. Sangaride believes that Atys has devoted himself to Cybelle, and she decides that she will marry Celanus out of duty. No reason for this sudden change of affairs is given. On learning of Sangaride's resolve, Atys surrenders completely to his love, and the lovers use Cybelle's power to meet secretly. Sangaride's father announces her approaching wedding in another scene of festivity which is overshadowed by the knowledge of the audience that the joyfulness of the participants is based on a false premise. Atys halts the celebration with the announcement that Cybelle forbids the wedding. This final act of treason is the climax of the play.

The fifth act brings the results of the action in act four. Cybelle tells Celanus of the perfidiousness of the lovers and invites him to aid her in securing vengeance. Atys is crazed by the vision of a monster whom he sacrifices to the goddess. Cybelle brings him to his senses so that he may see that he has murdered Sangaride. Atys takes his own life, and Cybelle is punished because she cannot follow him in death for she is immortal.

The over-all progression of the five acts is shown in the spectacles. In act one, Cybelle's coming to earth; act two, Atys becomes her priest; act three, the slumber; act four, the interrupted celebration of Sangaride's engagement; and in act five, her sacrifice and the death of Atys. While some of the plays are more closely woven than others, all of them proceed according to a similar basic plan. Since the spectacles were regulated by Lully and reflect the structure of the plot, it can be seen that the playwright and the composer worked together very closely, and it is this cooperation which gives strong dramatic progression to the *tragédie lyrique.*

Quinault portrays character by means of showing his heroes and heroines in a variety of situations, through their thoughts spoken in monologues, through commentary by the chorus and other characters, and through contrast with baser individuals.

Amadis provides an excellent example of how Quinault proceeds to portray character. Amadis is introduced in the prologue by Urgande who describes him as the greatest of French heroes (except Louis XIV). He is shown in the first act as the faithful but unhappy lover to whom Florestan reacts. Florestan tells Corisande that it is partially because of nobility of Amadis that he, himself, must seek glory. Some doubt is cast on the constancy of Amadis by Oriane, but both Florestan and Corisand doubt that Amadis could ever be faithless or a dissimulator. Arcabonne shows him to be magnanimous by her description of his rescue of her. Arcalaüs hates the hero because Amadis is devoted to destroying evil. Amadis cannot be conquered by arms or by evil spells in his fight with Arcalaüs, for only beauty, good, and the simulated form of Oriane are able to overcome him. In the final act Amadis is judged worthy to break the enchantment of the arch of true lovers and enter the forbidden chamber as the result of the perfection of his character. By placing Amadis first in one situation, then in another, and by having all the other characters react to him and express their thoughts of him, Quinault presents Amadis as the gallant hero, faithful and constant in love, without weakness, valiant in battle and acting always from magnanimity.

Arcalaüs balances and conflicts with the character of Amadis. In every circumstance he expresses only wicked and base feelings. Not only does Arcalaüs set out to destroy Amadis because of the goodness in the latter's character, but also he is so evil that he takes pleasure in seeing the suffering of others. Arcalaüs thus serves to provide an antagonist for Amadis, and at the same time he places the character of Amadis in relief.

Oriane is the female representative of nobility of character. She is prepared to accomplish her duty in spite of her own feelings. Though she is jealous, she does not think of revenge, but rather of living her life as well as she can. She tries to conquer her feelings but shows her love is constant when confronted by the supposed body of Amadis. It is interesting to note that in the romance from which the opera was taken, Oriane is a much stronger character—sprightly, filled with wit and cleverness, and showing much daring and initiative in bringing about the all too rare meetings between herself and Amadis. He, also, has become less the knight and more the lover.

Arcabonne contrasts with Oriane in much the same way that Arcalaüs contrasts with Amadis. Her love can be turned to hatred through jealousy and, like her brother, she enjoys the sight of suffering and lives to combat goodness.

Florestan and Corisande are less completely delineated since they are subsidiary characters. They serve as dramatic presences which permit Amadis and Oriane to stand out more clearly. Basically they are good, true and constant, but since Florestan is prevented from breaking the enchantment, it is clear that he is less perfect than Amadis.

The good magicians, Urgande and Alquif, serve the purpose of the *deus ex machina*. Since they are protectors of Amadis they underscore the nobility of his character, and it is through their intervention that Amadis and Oriane receive their final reward.

Portrayal of character in the other *tragédies lyriques* is accomplished in essentially the same way. The protagonist receives the most complete delineation, and the personal character traits of the subsidiary characters are chosen in such a way as to contrast with that of the protagonist, or to reveal his character through their reactions to him. If the protagonists seem unreal, it is not through lack of skill on the part of Quinault, but rather because the characters whom he has chosen to portray are themselves unreal by present-day standards.

It is the strength of dramatic progression, combined with the excellence of character portrayal, which make the libretti of Quinault able to survive the compromises required by musical setting of his plays. The simplicity and obviousness of his verse would be defeating weaknesses in a stage play, but they are virtues in a libretto where musical setting must be allowed to aid and intensify the expression of feeling and thought. The presentation of a single theme in a variety of stories leads to a certain monotony and it was, at least in part, concession to the taste of his public. Quinault was a *précieux*, and there is some truth in the accusation that he made tender love and not passion the motive for all acts. There is some question as to whether or not this was done on purpose. LeCerf de la Viéville states that Lully once demonstrated to a party of friends that he could write ferocious and terrifying music as well as the charming and melancholy[25] so that it may be that Quinault and Lully were portraying restrained sentiments on purpose. Beside the characters of Racine those of Quinault seemed lifeless and were so criticized by his contemporaries. However, on the whole, Quinault's libretti are some of the best examples of a good compromise between the elements of drama and music with the faults and virtues of all compromises.

Lully's Use of Recitative in Setting Quinault's *Libretti*

Given the importance of the drama and delineation of character in the *tragédies lyriques* it is obvious that the musical settings of dialogue and monologue would be important. The Italian concept of opera, with its emphasis on aria, is inappropriate to such plays as those written by Quinault and Lully. Scenes in French opera could not be built on sequences of recitative-aria, and it is noteworthy that there are very few arias in the Lully operas. Consistent through-composition of dialogue and monologue inevitably leads to the monotony which was criticized in early Florentine monody, and Lully was a performer who understood very well that the first rule of theater is not to bore the audience. He developed a variety of manners of setting scenes in which the main element is dialogue or monologue. Throughout any given scene the style of setting remains much the same, and it is possible to group them according to type.

⊛ Recitative-dialogue   Scene 2

Scenes in which the action is carried forward or character is revealed are by far the most common type, and these are set in a style which moves freely from *parlando* into more melodic recitative. Recitative-dialogue will be the term used to distinguish such scenes from other forms of recitative. Sometimes a short song is interpolated into the action, sometimes the scene terminates with a duo or trio. Often the scene is set in recitative throughout but with small sections being semistructured through the repetition, by the musician, of lines of poetry. Such sections are set in a more lyrical style of recitative though the speech may begin in *parlando* style. Above all, rhythm and pitch are used to indicate inflections of voice, while meter changes serve to vary the rapidity of delivery. Scenes of explanation, recognition, love scenes, arguments, and comic episodes are all set in this style. With the exception of *Thésée, Atys,* and *Roland* the *tragédies lyriques* begin with such scenes.

The second scene of the third act of *Psyché* may be cited as an example. The dialogue spoken by both characters moves freely from *parlando* to melodic style. There are two semistructured parts but no true songs. The purpose of the scene is the persuasion of Psyche by Venus to attempt to discover who her lover is, and much of the dialogue is set in such a way as to indicate expression to be given to the individual speeches.[26]

An example of a scene which is more structured from a musical point of view may be found in *Alceste* I, 4. Straton has been told by Lychas that Céphise is no longer exclusively his. In the scene between Céphise and Straton, the nymph argues with her former lover that he has no valid complaint, it is he who first taught her inconstancy. The text gives no indication of structuring up to the last couplet, but throughout the scene Lully used the device of repeating lines of the speeches in order to achieve both emphasis and formal structure. He has also included two arioso passages and concludes the scene with a duet.[27]

In recitative-dialogue scenes there is generally one actor and one reactor though sometimes the latter may be replaced by two characters who sing together. The melodic settings of text move with suppleness from *parlando* style into arioso style and back so that songs, when they occur, do not seem like sudden breaks in the musical continuity. Meter changes are frequent and aid in producing a more natural declamation of the text.

Scene I - No. 8

Recitative-monologue

The dramatic monologue of the *tragédie* is also found in the *tragédie lyrique* and will be called recitative monologue. These settings occupy an entire scene and are marked "RECIT" in printings made under Lully's supervision. They are used for several purposes: to introduce a character, to permit the audience to enter into the heart of an actor and discover his motivation, and to show a decisive change in direction of the story. Recitative-monologue scenes are much rarer than recitative-dialogue but all are of key importance. *Atys* begins in this way as does *Roland*. The recitative-monologue is similar in purpose to the *récit* which preceded each large section of a *ballet de cour* to explain the action. The recitative-monologue has been expanded so that action takes place within it, accompanied by a change of heart in the person who is speaking.

Roland IV, 2 is an example. In this scene Roland, while awaiting the arrival of Angelique, discovers the inscriptions on the rocks which tell him that she has eloped with Medor. At first, he cannot believe what he reads, but his doubt grows bit by bit. The sound of a distant village festival comes to his ears, and he decides to seek certainty from the shepherds. Recitative-monologue scenes are the only examples of recitative accompanied by the full orchestra in the *tragédies lyriques.* All other recitative is accompanied only by the continuo group or by the continuo with two treble instruments. The orchestra is used as a structuring element in recitative-monologue, and there is occasional melodic imitation between it and the voice. As in dialogue, the setting of speech in the monologue is varied moving freely from *parlando* to song-like settings with passages in which declamation is clearly indicated through rhythm and meter changes as well as pitch. Since recitative-monologue scenes are often relatively long, structuring of various sorts is present.[28]

Scene-complex

Recitative is also used by Lully in spectacular scenes which employ a number of soloists as well as the chorus, or double chorus. Battle scenes, funeral scenes, celebrations, sacrifices to the gods, and the wedding scenes which are so often the finales, all are based on exclamations which are the active factor and which enable the audience to follow the scene unfolding before them on the stage. The term scene-complex has been used to described such scenes. In the scene-complex main actors sing in recitative, the chorus is used as a character, reacting and chanting, frequently repeating words and phrases in a ritornello fashion in answer to the main actors, while the orchestra underscores the chorus and plays alone to accompany action. Such scenes have no typical structure since each one is dependent on an individual situation. Musical coherence is achieved in various ways such as the use of a repeated bass, an actual chaconne, and sometimes through the proportionate length of sequences given to soloists, orchestra, and choruses.

Persée, IV, 3 provides a good example of the variety obtained through use of different mediums in the scene-complex. It opens with a short musical prelude scored for the full orchestra followed by a trio deploring the cruel fate of Andromède. A single character then asks why she is being sacrificed, and it is explained that Junon demands it. Thus far the vocal parts are in *parlando* style.   The chorus enters as a commentator and is interrupted by frequent solo exclamations. Andromède's former fiance comments that for his part he would rather see her devoured by a monster than happy in the arms of another. Mérope reacts in astonishment to this assertion.   Phinée then sings a simple air on the same theme accompanied by two violins and continuo. This song melts into *parlando* style as Phinée resolves to bide his time.[29]

The basis of this scene is recitative mixed with spectacle, but in the concluding scene of the same act, the most important element is spectacle.   Persée slays the monster to the accompaniment of the orchestra interspersed with choral declamation followed by the celebration of his victory.   Recitative is limited to short interjections between orchestral sections and dances.

Summary and Conclusions

In summary, the *tragédie lyrique* of Lully and Quinault is a composite of music and drama so intricately interwoven that neither element plays a dominant role.   Rather, the two elements are combined in such a way that they complement each other.   The text is conceived as a vehicle not only to express a story but also to portray the concept of love and glory as seen by the French aristocratic public of the late seventeenth century.   The lives and deeds of heroes and heroines of Greek and Roman mythology and medieval romances are transformed to this end.   Scenes of a spectacular nature are incorporated in answer to the necessity for theatrical variety but are always the result of dramatic progression and are heightened by character portrayal.   Dramatic progression is obtained through the use of a large number of scenes in recitative-dialogue, while the motivation of characters and scenes showing changes in the direction of the action are set in recitative-monologue. Since the spectacles have meaning and relevance to the drama, understanding of the action in scene-complexes depends on interjections and exclamations in recitative.   Lully and Quinault fashioned both text and music to serve a dramatic ideal of their own conception which, while it borrowed elements from *tragédie,* machine play, *ballet de cour,* and Italian opera, was unique in its processes, its internal structure, its textual and musical techniques, and its form.

NOTES

[1]Will Durant, *The Story of Civilization*, Vol. VIII: *The Age of Louis XIV* (New York: Simon and Schuster, Inc., 1963), p. 30.

[2]LeCerf de la Viéville, "Vie de Lully," *Revue Musicale*, VI (January, 1925), 118.

[3]See p. 138 ff.

[4]Paul Bénichou, *Man and Ethics* (Garden City, N.Y.:   Anchor Books, 1971).

[5]Ibid., pp. 4-5.

[6]Jean-Baptiste Lully, *Oeuvres Complètes*, Les Opéras, Vol. 1, ed. by Henry Prunières (Paris: Editions de la Revue musicale, 1930), p. 89.

[7]Ibid., p. 169.

[8]Lully, ibid., Vol. 2, p. 301.

[9]Ibid., p. 302.

[10]Ibid., p. xiv.

[11]Robert Graves, *The Greek Myths* (Baltimore, Maryland: Penguin Books, 1955), Vol. I, p. 366.

[12]Lully, *Bellérophon* (Paris: Christophe Ballard, 1714), p. 157.

[13]Ibid., p. 164.

[14]Henry Prunières, "Notice Historique," in Lully, *Oeuvres Complètes*, Les Opéras, Vol. III, no page number.

[15]This letter is printed with the prefatory material of the complete works, *Les Opéras*, III, with a dedicatory poem by la Fontaine who indicates that Louis XIV had chosen the subject, and with extremely complimentary comparisons of the character of Amadis to that of the King.

[16]See: John J. O'Connor, *Amadis de Gaule and Its Influence on Elizabethan Literature* (New Brunswick, N.J.:   Rutgers Press, 1970), chap. I, and Eugène Baret, *De l'Amadis de Gaule et de son influence sur les moeurs et la littérature au XVIe et au XVIIe siècle avec une notice bibliographique* (Paris: Librairie de Firmin-Didot Frères, Fils et Cie., 1873), chap. II.   Before O'Connor can demonstrate the influence of *Amadis* on English literature and life--Elizabeth I enjoyed being called "fair Orianna"--he was first compelled to show its pervasive influence in France.   Of the two studies, O'Connor's is the more comprehensive.

[17]Alfonso Lopes Vieira, *O Romance do Amadis, Reconstituçao do Amadis de Gaula dos Lobeiras* (Lisboa: Sociedad editora Portugal-Brasil, 1926).   The French translation of this work, by Phileas Lebesque, was used by Etienne Gros in his research on the *Amadis* of Quinault.   It is extremely difficult to find a copy of the entire Amadis cycle, and O'Connor very seriously doubts that anyone in modern days has been able to read the whole work.

[18]Nicholas de Herberay, Seigneur des Essarts, *Le Premier livre d'Amadis de Gaule*, published from the original edition by Hugues Vaganay (Paris: Librairie Hachette et Cie., 1918), passim.

[19]Baret, op. cit., pp. 101-10.

[20]Edouard Bourciez, *Les Moeurs polies et la littérature de cour sous Henri II* (Paris: 1886), p. 63, quoted by O'Connor, op. cit., p. 14.

[21]O'Connor, op. cit., p. 13.

[22]Ibid., pp. 14-15.

[23]Baret, op. cit., p. 188.

[24]Ibid., p. 189.

[25]la Laurencie, *Lully*, pp. 92-93.

[26]See Appendix V, Scene A, of the present work.

[27]See Appendix V, Scene B, of the present work.

[28]See Appendix V, Scene C, of the present work.

[29]See Appendix V, Scene D, of the present work.

CHAPTER IV

MUSIC IN SCENES BASED ON RECITATIVE

The basic unit of the *tragédie lyrique* is the scene, and the musical setting is determined by the type of scene being set. Each *tragédie lyrique* was examined, and it was found that all of them are constructed of five varieties of scenes, four of which are based on recitative. The fifth type will not be discussed since it includes airs and ensembles. Pieces of this sort constitute complete scenes in themselves and do not use recitative; therefore, they lie outside the present study. It also was found that musical settings of scenes were composed systematically and that once the basic type of scene has been determined, many elements which are to be found within it are predictable. Lully had evolved a structure and style for the setting of the *tragédies lyriques* within which he used great ingenuity. However, the various techniques used in the composition of recitative are the same from first to last. A general description of each type of scene follows, while a scene typical of each variety is given in modern notation in Appendix V.·

Recitative-Dialogue

Recitative-dialogue is most common of the four types of scenes in which recitative is found. Scenes of this sort are set in two basic manners: those which contain set songs and end with an ensemble, and those in which the setting moves freely between through-composed, *parlando* style recitative and semistructured *arioso* sections. Recitative-dialogue scenes of the latter type are generally found close to the beginning of acts. Their purpose is to advance the plot and to set up situations which must be resolved. Two or three such scenes may occur consecutively or they may be alternated with recitative-dialogue scenes which contain formally structured pieces. They also are found before and after scenes in which vocal ensembles occur, recitative-monologue scenes, or airs.

The musical settings of recitative-dialogue of this type tend to be in *parlando* style, but although the outlined triads and repeated notes of Italian recitative are present they are employed in such a manner as to indicate declamation and expression or emotion. Some semistructuring occurs within speeches whose basic style is *parlando* yet these passages do not achieve sufficient formal design to be called songs. Instead, the transition from *parlando* to *arioso* is scarcely perceptible.

The rhythmic setting of recitative-dialogue underscores the meaning of the speeches. This is accomplished through the use of frequently changing meters and rhythmic patterns. Lully writes some passages more explicitly than he does others, or perhaps he intends declamation to be differentiated from disputation, tender declaration and short exclamation. In any event there is a predominance of dactylic rhythmic patterns, particularly when simple declamation is desired. Speeches are set in such a manner that the end of a phrase or a line rarely coincides with the barline but on the contrary, a new speaker often begins to sing on the second of two eighth-notes on a weak beat. Speakers interrupt each other, words spoken in excitement are set to rapid rhythmic patterns, single words are emphasized by sudden changes in the tempo of speech, and pitches rise and fall with the changing rhythmic patterns so that the text is given the meaning desired by the composer.

Much has been said of the frequent meter changes in Lully's operas. It is certain that he intended both to accommodate the varying number of syllables per line in Quinault's poetry and also to indicate changes in the rapidity with which lines are delivered. While meter changes in songs are confined to sections in recitative, they often occur with each change of singer. They also are found in monologues.

The interpretation of meter signs used by Lully is not at all clear. Present usage of meter signatures was not yet fully established in the 1670's. The basic problem probably consists of determining the meaning of the breve in each of its varying contexts. Differing opinions likely will arise among scholars, and the topic will receive more extensive treatment when new critical editions are made.

Measures 50-70 of the transcribed scene from *Psyché* (Appendix V) are exemplary of the problem. Previous to measure 50, the meter sign given is the figure "3". Assuming present interpretation of the "C" which follows (♩ = ♩) there are no problems in resuming "3" in measure 54. The *alla breve* in measure 56 creates the difficulty for it is followed in measure 57 by "C" and in measure 58 by the figure "2" with a resumption of "C" in 59. The changes between "C" and "3" which follow all depend on the meaning of the *alla breve* and how far that sign should govern subsequent signs.

The following is proposed as a possible solution. The first two meter signs are interpreted according to present usage, quarter-note equals quarter-note and no change in tempo would occur. The *alla breve* indicates that subsequent meter changes are interpreted according to the proportional relationship of ♩. = ♩ . The *alla breve* to "C" means doubling the note-values while the "2" which follows indicates a change in emphasis rather than tempo. However, the possibility that Lully wished to indicate some quickening of tempo in this way should not be overlooked. The change from "C" to "3" in measure 65 could be interpreted either as $\jmath = \jmath\cdot$ or $\jmath = \jmath$ though the former seems more likely.

The foregoing is exemplary of the problems encountered, for in measure 75 of the same scene a sign of "2" follows "C"; however, each measure of duple time contains a total value of a single half-note, while in measure 77 the sign given is "3" and in measure 78, "C". In measure 80, "2" appears once more but this time the total note-value per measure is a · whole note.

It seems reasonable to state that each case would have to be considered individually, all of the possibilities examined, and, finally, the interpretation which assured the best delivery of the text should be adopted. In short, any performance of Lully's *tragédies lyriques* would require a full study of this matter.

The harmonic structure tends to bring out the expression of the words without the variety of the Italian idiom. Each scene is composed in a basic key, and transient modulations are used to obtain harmonic variety. Such key changes are rarely of longer duration that four or five measures and may be considered as elaborations of the basic key. This is the manner in which they are shown in the brackets in Appendix V. Most frequently, a single secondary key is used. When the basic key is major the alternate key is most often the supertonic minor. When the basic key is minor, the alternate key is most often the relative major. Transient modulations to other keys and momentary tonicizations of chords are often used for expressive purposes. Cross-relations are exploited to underline sharply contrasting feelings and are usually brought about the juxtaposition of major and minor triads built on the same root. Harmonic rhythm quickens at moments of increasing tension and at the approach to a strong cadence. Most chords are simple triads but Lully employs the minor seventh chord frequently to underscore moments of sorrow.

The semistructuring of passages in recitative-dialogue grows out of the *récit* of the *ballet de cour* where the *récits* were structured (two parts with repeats, and strophic) and where the composer frequently repeated the last line of the text to which he composed different music. Such repetition of lines was further developed by Lully so that semistructuring is based on any line or group of lines from a speech. Musically, sometimes the melody is retained, sometimes only the rhythm, and sometimes the second setting of the words is entirely different. Semistructuring of this sort provides variety and a relaxation from the *parlando* style.

The accompaniment of recitative-dialogue is restricted to the continuo. There is often an opening *ritournelle* scored for two violins and continuo, but the violins drop out when the vocal part begins. *Ritournelle* is the term Lully used to designate instrumental introductory pieces even though they almost never "return." They are invariably scored for two treble instruments and continuo. When Lully uses the entire orchestra for introductory pieces he calls them *préludes*, and these frequently contain material which is used later in the scene. The terms do not correspond in usage to the Italian names for instrumental pieces and, therefore, the French terminology is retained. Sometimes *ritournelles* are marked "*se joue deux fois*" in which event the repetition normally would be played softly. The continuo does not serve merely as harmonic underlining all of the time, but often through the use of chord inversions, a strong bass-line is obtained in which there are frequent passages in stepwise movement. Sometimes Lully writes entire scales in this way, extending over an eleventh or a twelfth. Such a bass-line would cause tension to mount as it ascends or tend to emphasize a feeling of finality as it descends and thus contribute to the general emotional expression of the text.

The second scene of the third act of *Psyché* consists entirely of recitative and contains only two short sections which are semistructured. These occur near the beginning (mm. 12-46) and within through-composed recitative (mm. 81-101). It is in this scene that *Psyché* is tempted by Venus to disobey her lover and try to discover who he is. The poetry is free verse; irregular meter prevails with three to thirteen feet per line, and there is no organized scheme of either meter or rhythm.

Recitative-dialogue scenes which contain set songs, duos, and semistructured passages differ from those which do not, both in musical setting and in purpose. They rarely appear at the beginning or at the end of an act, but rather they create variety in a series of dialogue scenes where a spectacle would be inappropriate. Such scenes effectively increase the tension and musical interest as spectacle scenes, or scene-complexes are approached.

The melodic structure of recitative-dialogue scenes which contain fixed forms is more varied than that of the recitative-dialogue scenes in which there are no fixed forms. Semistructuring occurs quite frequently, particularly in the speeches of the character whose melodic setting tends to be more nearly *arioso*. Rhythm and harmony are used in much the same way in all scenes.

The fixed forms contained in these scenes are clearly differentiated from the rest of the speeches. There are *rondeaux*, sung minuets, and other dance-forms with words. While the repetitions of lines in semistructured portions appear to have been the work of the composer, most often the verses for the set forms were conceived by the poet for that purpose. Frequently there are *arioso* passages for bass voice accompanied by two treble instruments, violins, flutes, or oboes depending on the identity of the character who sings. Raguenet describes the excellence of the bass singers of France saying that Italy has nothing to compare with them and Lully gives ample parts to basses.[1] Furthermore, the range of songs for female sopranos rarely is larger than a ninth, while bass parts usually are written with a range of a twelfth. Raguenet also says that there were no castratos in France,[2] and it should be noted that the great singer, Dumesnil, trained by Lully, was a male soprano.   The part of Amadis was written for him.

As   in   the   recitative-dialogue   without   set-songs,   the accompaniment is restricted to the continuo with the exception of the opening *ritournelle* and of the bass *arioso* passages. Frequently the singer continues to be accompanied by the three-part group after the semistructured passages are sung, while the speeches of the other character are accompanied by the continuo alone.

Act. 1, scene 4 of *Alceste* provides a good example of a recitative-dialogue containing set forms.   There are four semistructured passages and a final duet. This is the scene in which Straton accuses Céphise of infidelity and she agrees with his accusation.

The difference between the recitative-dialogue with set songs, terminating in an ensemble, and recitative-dialogue wherein only semistructuring occurs is not one of principle but of stress.   The emphasis in a recitative-dialogue scene which is mostly through-composed is on conversation, the declamation of individual words, and rapidly changing action. In the case of recitative-dialogue with set songs, the emphasis is on the semistructured portions of the scene, each of which is individually organized.   Conversation, interpretation of individual words, and changing feeling exist in both types of scenes, however, as does semistructuring.

Scene-complex

The scene-complex is distinguished from other types of scenes in the *tragédie lyrique* in that all the available media are used--soloists, single chorus, double choruses, small ensembles of solo voices, small orchestra, large orchestra, and the continuo--either singly or in varying combinations.   The final scenes of all *tragédies lyriques* are scene-complexes. Sometimes several scene-complexes occur in succession as, for example, in the fourth act of *Persée*. Scenes of this type can be either highly structured and unified musically or they can consist of suites of dances alternating with recitative, airs, duos, trios, and choral passages.   Since each scene-complex serves an individual dramatic purpose, the formal plan is different for each. The dramatic movement of the plot is kept before the audience through the use of exclamations and explanations cast in recitative.

The musical setting of recitative in the scene-complex does not differ from that used in dialogue. Melody, rhythm, and harmony are handled in the same fashion. Sometimes, however, after an exclamation is sung by a soloist, the same melody is harmonized and given to the chorus. Thereafter the passage may be used as is a *ritornello*, and it then becomes a factor in achieving formal structure. The accompaniment of scene-complexes depends on which group, or groups, are singing. Recitative accompaniment for soloists is generally restricted to the continuo just as it was in recitative-dialogue, while the full orchestra plays instrumental interludes, dances, and doubles the chorus. The small orchestra accompanies or doubles duets and trios of soloists, and in the mixing and alternating of the various groups of voices and instruments, Lully often uses *concertato* style.

When only a few lines of poetry are used to construct a scene-complex, the musical structuring tends to be more prominent than when there are many lines of poetry to be set. In the former instance there may be many dance suites and fixed vocal forms with *parlando* style recitative to connect the various events and instruct the audience in the course of the action. In battle scenes, sacrifices or celebrations, the forces of the opposing choruses, soloists, and orchestras are sometimes organized into *chaconnes*, combined with the *ritornello* design.

The *chaconne* in the final scene of *Amadis* is an example. For resources, Lully has the chorus, four soloists, the full orchestra, and the continuo group. Two recurring bass melodies are used:

The highest vocal part is constructed of resembling but not repetitive patterns consisting of two phrases four measures long the first of which ends with an open cadence, the second, closed. While the same type of thematic variation is used with the *chaconne* patterns as with the vocal soprano, or solo, pattern, there is insufficient variety to support a lengthy structure. The variety is supplied by contrasting textures. There is an underlying scheme based on the use of the two *chaconne* melodies.

I	II	I	II	I
60 mm.	16 mm.	88 mm.	16 mm.	32 mm.

Thus, the underlying scheme, in five parts, is arch-shaped, and is built around a long center section which resembles the beginning section and the ending section but is divided from them by two short sections based on a contrasting bass pattern. The form is shown graphically below.

Chaconne Pattern	Vocal Texture	Accompaniment
Part 1 (60 measures)		
3 entries of I	Full chorus	Full orchestra
4 1/2 entries of I	Solo chorus	Continuo group
Part 2 (16 measures)		
1 entry of II	Full chorus	Full orchestra
I entry of II	Solo chorus	Continuo group
Part 3 (88 measures)		
1 entry of I	Full chorus	Full orchestra
1 entry of I	Solo chorus	Continuo group
1 entry of I	Soloist	Continuo group
2 entries of I	Full chorus	Full orchestra
2 entries of I	Soloist	Continuo group
2 entries of I	Full chorus	Full orchestra
2 entries of I	Trio	Continuo group
Part 4 (16 measures)		
1 entry of II	Full chorus	Full orchestra
1 entry of II	Trio	Continuo group
Part 5 (32) measures)		
1 entry of I	Soloist	Continuo group
1 entry of I	Full chorus	Full orchestra
2 entries of I	Soloist	Continuo group

When there are many lines of poetry, recitative plays a much larger role. The chorus is present and is handled in the same manner, there are some elements of spectacle, and there may be some fixed vocal forms, but recitative is the major element.

Act IV, scene iii of *Persée* is an example of a scene-complex in which recitative predominates. In this scene it is announced that

Andromède must be sacrificed to a sea monster in order to appease the wrath of Junon. Lully requires a small orchestra, the full orchestra, an ensemble of three vocal soloists, the full chorus, and three main characters who sing individually. There are four main parts to the scene: in the first, the instrumental introduction is followed by a choral exclamation; in the second, an announcement is made in recitative; the third is built largely on the first; and the fourth is a dialogue which finishes with a semistructured piece. In addition to this, vocal groups echo exclamations of soloists and such repetitions are also structuring elements. Due to the differing media used, sectionalization in scene-complexes tends to be more clear-out, for recitative retains its characteristic accompaniment by the continuo. Most important, scene-complexes are all comparatively spectacular in the *tragédie lyrique*, but such spectacles are woven into the main fabric of the drama through the use of recitative so that the action is not entirely halted but merely slowed down, and the dramatic impact is heightened through spectacle.

Recitative-monologue

Recitative-monologue, that is, a scene which is sung throughout by a single character, is a form of declamation which is chanted or sung and can be traced back to antiquity. One of the reasons for the effectiveness of monologue lies in the potential concentration of heightened emotions when only one person is on stage. The *récit* of the *ballet de cour* is the direct ancestor of the monologue. It consists of a long speech, essential to the drama, in which there is either an explanation of action which takes place off-stage, or an important discovery causing a change of heart to take place in the speaker. Recitative-monologue scenes can occur anywhere within an act but are most likely to be found either at the beginning or framed between scenes of recitative-dialogue.

The recitative-monologue contains both semistructured sections and parts which are through-composed. The accompaniment for such scenes is always the full orchestra. In the transcribed example form *Roland* (Appendix V) there is also a short passage for small orchestra, but this is exceptional. There is no other medium than the single voice through which variety can be obtained; therefore, the orchestra plays an extremely important role.

The monologue sung by Roland in Act IV, scene ii of the drama of that name contains the moment in which he discovers, unbelieving, that Angelique has eloped with Medor, the event which subsequently causes his madness. The setting combines highly structured sequences with a long central section which is through-composed. As is the case in all of the monologue recitatives of the *tragédies lyriques* the full orchestra is used both for instrumental interludes and to accompany the actor who is singing.

Just as the main stress in the recitative-dialogue is different from that of the scene-complex, the emphasis in recitative-monologue is different from that of the other two types. The purpose of the scenes set in this manner by Lully is to dramatize a major event, often a change of heart in the protagonist which changes the course of the action in the rest of the drama. For this reason, expressive setting of the decisive portion of the text is the most important element in the recitative-monologue. Again, it is not a question of a completely different type of setting but rather one of emphasis. Those elements which characterize the setting of recitative by Lully—dramatizing individual words, setting exclamations apart from the rest of the text, providing a general atmosphere, and keeping the story moving through the musical means of melody, harmony, rhythm and scoring--are found in all scenes in which recitative is used.

Musical Characteristics Common to All Four Types of Scene

Many of the musical techniques which Lully used in setting scenes are shared regardless of the type of scene involved. Among these is his use of musical elements to give expression to the text, and it should be noted that in many instances the composer actually changes the meaning of the words.

It often has been said that Lully observed poetic line, rhyme, and *caesurae* in his settings, but this is not the essential element in the Lully recitative. Through a subtle use of musical elements, Lully actually sets diction in such a way that it is not words which are put to music, but rather the actor's interpretation of the words. Interruptions in train of thought, hastening and slowing of speech for expressive purposes, excitement, disappointment, anger, surprise, scorn, joy, hope—all nuances are written into the music. Nowhere is this more true than in scenes of recitative-monologue where Lully demonstrates the consumate knowledge of the performer who speaks aloud and lives with all of the words before attempting to interpret the nuances of meaning. This is what Lully set to music, not merely the observance of poetic form or linguistic cadence, and in the most important speeches of his *tragédies lyriques* he shows himself to be a master actor.

The central section of the monologue from *Roland* (mm.128-192) provides a good example. It contains thirty-three lines of poetry set a seventy-four measures of music, entirely through-composed, without repetition or any other type of formal organization. The text provides the framework which Lully has set, phrase by phrase, in an expressive manner. This is the crucial point in the play. Roland discovers that

Angelique has inscribed her love for Medor on the rocks. At first he believes that she is dissimulating for he has never heard of Medor. When he reads of Medor's joy at obtaining his fondest desire, he becomes more doubtful. LeCerf de la Viéville said that Lully memorized each *tragédie lyrique* completely and spok? the words aloud after which he improvised the music to the accompaniment of the harpsichord until he was satisfied with the results. He quotes Lully as having said "Mon récitatif n'est fait que pour parler." This passage from *Roland* demonstrates his words. The melody, if such it can be called, of the singer is a *tour de force* in the musical setting of diction. To appreciate fully the ability of Lully to understand the art of declamation it is necessary to read aloud these lines of poetry, allowing the inflections of the voice to rise and fall with approximately the intervals of the written notes. As an actor, Lully knew how to increase tension by raising the pitch of the voice and how to release it by letting the pitch drop. All of these devices are allied to express the violently shifting emotions of Roland.

Roland's speech begins slowly with the orchestra accompanying (mm.118-123). He sings "Voyons tout" with falling inflection and then cries out in amazement (m. 124). The pitch is an octave higher and the tempo changes written in note-values are rapid. The line descends as he recognizes her handwriting (mm. 125-128), but another leap of an octave sets off the exclamation *"Ciel!"* (m. 128). He reads Angelique's inscription in measured tones (mm. 132-136), speaks more rapidly as he voices his suspicion (mm. 136-137), followed by another exclamation to a downward leap of a fifth as he recognizes her ingratitude. He wonders, more slowly, if his suspicions are not an unmerited offense to her, then reads that Medor has her heart. He muses over the meaning of the words, speaking more rapidly, and the pitch rises a perfect fifth by stepwise movement and repeated notes over four measures as he reassures himself that Angelique has not dared to confess that he is a master of her heart (mm. 153-156).

Slowly, with emphasis, he says "C'est pour moi seul qu'elle soupire" (mm. 160-162). The note-values are doubled in length for this declaration, but he immediately rushes into the statement that she has told him so and he is certain of her faith--to note-values which are halved. He reads further and shouts in his dismay (mm. 168-170). The pitch first drops a perfect fifth, followed by a quarter rest, then an upward leap of a sixth to the high E-flat dramatizes the word *"Ciel!"* of half-note valued tied across a barline. The violins play a descending scale from A-flat (m. 172), and Roland reads Medor's inscription continuing the descending movement a full octave. Outraged at what he has read, he exclaims in a rapid and excited way that Medor, not he, is Angelique's true love, but immediately he denies it. His first cry "Non", is set off by the upward leap of a sixth, prolonged as a quarter-note value and separated from the rest of the speech by an eighth rest (m. 187). The final two bars are slightly slower, and his voice falls as he says that surely someone who is envious of him has tried to blacken the reputation of the one he loves in order to trouble his peace of mind.

The orchestral accompaniment provides a sonorous harmonic background, almost entirely chordal, with a single measure of interplay between the violins and the voice (m. 130). The harmonic rhythm is slow and measured except at cadence points and expressive moments. For example, the mounting scale passage (mm. 153-156) is underscored and its tension enhanced by a doubling of the speed of the harmonic rhythm. The same thing occurs when Roland sings that Angelique has told him that she sighs for him alone (mm. 160-162). Most notably the harmonic rhythm increases in speed in the final twelve bars to underline Roland's increasing doubt. Thus, the accompaniment serves the purpose of increasing the expressive quality of the setting while permitting the voice to stand out in relief against the orchestra. This technique is used by Lully to set speeches in which the emotional fluctuations of a character must be made clear to the audience.

In sequences of conversational speeches there are certain elements which tend to bind the dialogue together. Poetically, rhyming patterns overlap from section to section and speech to speech while musically, cadences are accomplished before the end of one speech so that the second speaker begins to sing without a harmonic change. The speakers follow each other very rapidly and, indeed, in some instances they interrupt each other. Measures 30-43 of Act I, scene iii from *Alceste* demonstrates the manner in which Lully set conversation. In this instance Lully has portrayed an argument between two former lovers. Straton's first speech is practically blurted out as he accuses Céphise of being unfaithful to him (mm. 30-33). The three lines of poetry contain 9, 13, and 12 syllables, and the rhythm of the setting is mostly in sixteenth notes. The music is fitted to the poetry in such a way that the ends of lines fall on the third quarter of each beat and the next line begins immediately, just as a person who does not wish to be interrupted runs one phrase into another until he runs out of breath. The melody of the first line ascends a seventh by means of two leaps of a fourth separated by repeated notes and a short ornamental figure while the second-line melody is static, confined within a tritone. The third line begins high and descends a full octave and a fifth to the final lugubrious note, first by a descending scale passage, then by two downward leaps of a fifth separated by repeated notes.

Céphise answers slowly, measure 33, her six syllables almost murmured, require a full measure of comparison with Straton's twelve syllables in the preceding measure. The harmony also lingers on the secondary dominant and resolves only on her last syllable. The melody descends a third stepwise.

Straton interrupts her, for he is joyfully deluding himself in the belief that she is denying his accusation. In a melodic pattern constructed of the outlined dominant triad and ending with an upward leap of a fourth, he shouts out his certainty that Lychas was trying to fool him. The harmony moves with the voice in an authentic cadence.

Céphise patiently reiterates (mm. 36-38) "Lychas est peu discret. . ." in the same slow rhythm as the first time, then pauses for the length of an eighth rest before saying "d'avoir dit mon secret." The rhythm is arranged to stress the word "dit" to indicate that Lychas' indiscretion consisted not of what he had done but of what he had said. The melodic motion is largely conjunct in the first line (six syllables) while the second line (also six syllables) is set by outlining a triad and then bringing in the authentic cadence.

This declaration outrages Straton whose shout of anger is followed by a series of sixteenth notes compressing two lines of poetry (each of which contains thirteen syllables) into two measures. He still is speaking twice as rapidly as Céphise. The melodic contour moves upward a fifth in mostly stepwise fashion with several repeated notes in the first line, m. 38, while the melody of the second line descends a full octave, mostly by skips, with many repeated notes. The occasional eighth notes are placed so that spoken in the rhythm prescribed by Lully the syllabic emphasis produces exactly the expression desired by the composer. "What! It is TRUE? You make no EXCUSE? You are unfaithful like THAT without being EMBARRASSED?"

The harmony underlines Straton's feelings. An A-major triad is juxtaposed (m. 38) with the F-major tonic so well established in the previous phrase. Since the C-sharp appears in the bass, the false relation is all the more apparent. The key of G minor having been assumed in this manner (A major triad = V of V in G), the confirming cadence follows, and the speech ends on the dominant with a shift to triple meter.

Céphise is becoming agitated and starts speaking more rapidly. The melodic range (mm. 41-43) is restricted to a perfect fourth. The rhythm is particularly striking in that Lully has underlined the basic irony of the words. While the words "reason" and "treason" are stressed (each is on the first beat of a measure and has a quarter-note value) the word "undeceive" (désabuse) is cut unduly short giving it a comical twist.

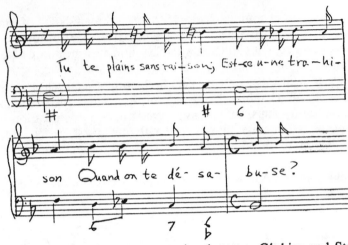

Tu te plains sans raison; Est-ce u-ne tra-hi-son Quand on te dé-sa-bu-se?

The purpose of the conversation between Céphise and Straton is to prolong a momentary pause in the main action while underlining the difference in character between Céphise and Alceste. The recitative-dialogue scene from *Psyché* serves to advance the action, and the last series of speeches (mm. 101-124) demonstrate Lully's manner of moving action forward by musical means.

In *Psyché* the text is set in a straight-forward fashion with natural rise and fall of pitch and few instances of underlining or changes in meaning of words through musical means. The rhythmic setting also tends to be clear-cut and consists either of the dactylic pattern or notes of equal value except at ends of phrases. The tempo is slowed or speeded up by meter changes to approximate speech. Deep emotional impact is not sought in such passages, for it would tend to slow down the movement of the action. Lully's setting of this conversation is designed to hasten the moment of action once the decision to disobey her lover has been made.

Psyché cries out, and in a speech of rising intensity begs Venus to help her. All of the musical elements underscore the forward movement of this speech. The opening exclamation "Ah!" (m. 103) is followed by a rest and a downward leap of a sixth after which it ascends a diminished octave in mostly stepwise movement with a single break in the continuity. There are a number of repeated notes. The rhythm also reflects the growing excitement of Psyché, for measure by measure her speech becomes more rapid through the use of meter changes or varied rhythmic organization (mm. 103-107). The harmonic rhythm underlines the forward movement by progressively faster chord changes while the return to B-flat comes in the final measure.

The scene closes rapidly. Venus requires a bit more convincing after which she shows Psyché where her lover sleeps, gives her a lamp with which to see him, and quickly retires, thus ending the scene. The first speeches (mm. 107-108) are set off from each other by eighth rests, and the notes and rhythm are such that they might be spoken as written and give the impression of natural speech. The harmonic rhythm is slow; the pattern of chords is based on primary triads of the key.

Psyché breaks in with her final speech of persuasion, again an ascending melodic line, intensified by a modulation to C-minor (mm. 109-111). . Venus appears to pause, then each word is set with changing rhythmic pattern or meter to emphasize to Psyché that the latter's desire is about to be fulfilled. "Entrez" (m. 113) is set off with rests, and "Goutez" is repeated (mm. 115-116) and emphasized further by melodic leaps in a passage where repeated notes and stepwise motion prevail. The G minor chord is juxtaposed with G major as Venus reveals the place where Amour sleeps again demonstrating Lully's use of major and minor contrast to express a sudden change. Modulation back to B-flat major is through the circle of fifths. As Venus gives the lamp to Psyché, her voice mounts in pitch over a solid cadence to the tonic as if all difficulties had been resolved.

Psyché murmurs her thanks on repeated notes of equal rhythmic value with a final downward inflection of her voice (m. 119). Venus retires abruptly, but her excitement at her success in tempting Psyché is betrayed by her voice for the speech quickens with a change of meter and ascends scalewise to form an arch with the final cadential material (mm. 120-124).

The monologue of Idas, Act IV, scene iv (mm. 30-58) in *Persée* is like the final exchange of words between Venus and Psyché. The purpose in the latter case was to advance the action rapidly and bring the scene to a close. In the scene from *Persée* the purpose is the exposition of a situation so that the audience may understand what is taking place. Lully had no interest in slowing the pace of the speech; therefore, it is not individual words which are set, or emotions which are prolonged through musical means. Changes in pitch and tempo are used to approximate the manner in which such a speech would be declaimed or spoken. It should be noted particularly that while Lully observes the natural rise and fall of pitch, and perhaps overuses the dactylic pattern, the element which gives the most vivid expression to his setting of recitative is his selection of vital words and the varying twists of meaning which he gives to them. This technique is to be found in all Lully recitative. Examples are numerous, and the manner of accomplishing such word setting is varied. Sometimes unusual intervals are used to express emotion as for example when Phinée says, "It is from MY arms that love tears her? It is Persée. . ."

The intervals of the melody are quite unusual in comparison to those used in the rest of the scene. In this manner, Lully has emphasized Phinée's hatred for *Persée* without interrupting the rapid flow of dialogue.

In other instances, words are set off from the remainder of a speech by rests. This is particularly true of exclamations such as "Non," in *Roland* and "Entrez," in *Psyché*.

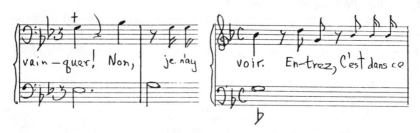

In both cases, the expression of the word is further enhanced by the melodic interval used.

Changing note values have been used to vary the tempo of a speech in order to increase the emphasis on emotionally charged words and phrases. For example, in Psyché's speech (mm. 57-72) the prevailing note-values are eighth and sixteenth-notes; however, the final syllable of "ce refus" (m. 62) is a quarter-note which interrupts the rhythmic flow. The words "je l'aime" are set off in a similar manner (m. 63), while the words "qu'il ose rebuter" are set entirely in eighth-notes and further underscored by a momentary tonicization of the C minor triad.

Lully also uses musical means to alter the meaning of the text. In *Psyché* Venus sings, "Vous dont l'amour est si pur et si tendre" ("You whose love is so tender and pure").

The words "amour," "pur et si tendre" are set in relief through prolongation, and the ornament on "et" could be slightly exaggerated to lend a sarcastic nuance to the phrase. Lully has used musical means to reverse completely the meaning of the text. It would be possible for an actress to deliver these lines as Quinault wrote them in a perfectly sincere, sympathetic manner. That is one possible interpretation. However, when Lully had finished setting them as he did, sarcasm is clearly indicated.

This example is in the context of a semistructured section showing that Lully did not restrict expressive settings of individual words to *parlando* recitative. Indeed, as Raguenet has stated, it is difficult to differentiate between recitative and air in French opera.[3] The reason for this is that the basic material of which they are constructed is the same. Outlined triads, repeated notes, and scale passages are arranged to express whatever meaning the composer desired, while rhythm and harmony are used to further enhance the effect. Often two characters speak in different speeds, particularly at the beginning of scenes, thus showing the greater agitation of one of them. Changing tempi within speeches are also used to depict changing moods and emotions. Harmony also underscores feeling mostly through changes in the rapidity of the movement of harmonic rhythm. Chord changes become more rapid when the speaker becomes excited, although the approach to cadence points is also habitually brought out in the same manner.

Another harmonic means of underlining expression is the juxtaposition of a major triad with its parallel minor to show an abrupt change in emotion. There are numerous instances. In the scene from *Psyché* mentioned above, the cadence at the word "tendresse" (m. 74 is to C major, but the C minor triad follows immediately as Venus exclaims "Ah!"). The G minor triad is juxtaposed with G major as Venus reveals the place where Amour sleeps. Often the scoring is made to cause a cross-relation as in *Alceste* (m. 79) where the contrast is once again between a G minor and a G major triad, and the placing of B natural in the continuo part makes the clash even more evident.

A less obvious means of depicting emotional change is the substitution of a different key from that used most often as an elaboration of the basic key of a scene. An instance occurs in *Psyché* (mm. 91-93) accompanying a speech in which Psyché begs Venus to relieve her suspense. The basic key of the scene is B-flat major, and the tonal atmosphere used for varying the harmonic structure is the relative key of G minor. These measures, however, are quite clearly in the relative minor.

In other instances a harmonic progression is used to express feelings. For example, when Roland cries out "Ciel!" (m. 128), the word is underscored by the irregular movement of V to V-of-V. Most notable is the use of the Neapolitan, a complete negation of the tonic, when Roland says that Angelique has told him she is his. This gesture would well have been lost on the audience were it not for the effective use of this chord, a rare occurrence in the *tragédies lyriques*. It should be stressed that for the most part elaboration on the tonic by use of several measures cast in an alternate key is used for musical variety rather than for structuring or the expression of emotion. This is demonstrated by measures 128-192 in the scene from *Roland*. Nine modulations take place in the following order: C minor, E-flat major, C minor, G major, C minor, E-flat major, C minor, E-flat major, G major, and C. minor. C minor is first maintained for thirty measures after which five key changes occur in rapid succession (4 m., 3 m., 3 m., 3 m., 5 m). Another extended section in C minor (22 mm.) is followed by two rapid changes (4 m. and 2); therefore, no structuring pattern is established, nor are the modulations used to express shifts in emotion for the most dramatic portion of the speech is in the second long section in C minor.

Structuring within scenes is achieved by different means. In recitative-dialogue scenes, the interspersion of semistructured portions gives variety to conversation, while in recitative-monologue instrumental interludes serve the double purpose of binding the structure together and creating variety through the use of a different medium. In the scene-complex, structuring is most often achieved through the use of several media used in alternation and repeating short phrases in a *ritornello* fashion.

The semistructured portions of recitative-dialogue are built on repetition of lines of poetry chosen by the composer. No plan is followed regularly either as to the repetition of lines or the musical setting of the poetry. Two examples taken from the scene from *Alceste* are diagrammed below showing how Lully proceeded.

Measures 45-76

POETRY		MUSIC
1 (6 feet)		a
2 (7 feet)	A	a'
1		a
2	A	a'
3 (8 feet)		b
4 (9 feet)	B	c
4		d
3		e
4	C	c'
4		f

The speech might just as well have been set in *parlando* style and, therefore, the repetition of lines is the work of the composer. Furthermore, Lully did not repeat the music according to the poetry but rather inserted new settings thus giving different formal structure to the music.

Measures 117-148

POETRY		MUSIC
1 (9 feet)		a
1	A	a'
2 (15 feet)		b
3 (5 feet)		c
3	B	c'
4 (8 feet)		d
3		c"
4	B'	d'
4		d"

A comparison of the organization of these two songs shows that the procedure used is similar but that great variety is possible. The melodies of "a" and "a'" also demonstrate Lully's ability to construct thematic material which is related without exact repetition. The rhythmic setting of the two phrases is the same, and the melodic contour is similar but there is no actual repetition of notes. Nor is there sequential repetition.

The large number of semistructured portions in this scene from *Alceste* demonstrate Lully's ingenuity in giving musical structure to a passage without actually writing a song. The basic principle, as shown above, is the repetition of a line, or fragment of a line, or poetry while altering the musical setting in any of a number of ways, both melodic and rhythmic. Each semistructured passage, though it follows the basic principle, is individually conceived. No technique ever becomes a mere formula.

In contrast to the songs which preceded it, the final piece of this scene is a duet based on only three lines of poetry (mm. 148-172). The first line (six feet) is repeated five times to form a section; the second line (six feet), and the third (seven feet) form a unit which is repeated three times after which the first section returns giving an over-all A B A form. The poetry contains a device which occurs quite frequently in the *tragédies lyriques*. The two characters are maintaining opposing views, and in order for each to keep his position, Quinault alters only two words in the same verse:

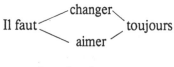

Les plus douces amours

Interestingly, this duet contains one of the rare instances in which Lully violates the natural movement and feeling of the French language. There is no obvious reason except the maintenance of the dotted rhythmic pattern.

Les plus dou-ces a-mours   Sont les a-mours nou-vel-les.

The final cadence of section B is brought about with a change in the rhythm which suddenly brings everything back into place.

Sont les a-mours nou-vel-les.

The other form of internal structuring found frequently in the four types of scenes is the use of a fixed bass pattern. The *chaconne* combined with *ritornello* design has already been discussed. In addition to such complex forms Lully makes use of ground basses in many other instances. The orchestral interlude from *Roland* (mm. 77-88) is an example. There seems to be no formal structuring until the continuo part is examined. The first four bars consist of the minor *chaconne* pattern followed by its inversion, while the final group of four measures is based on a variation of the Romanesca.

As a dancer and composer of instrumental music Lully was very familiar with ground basses and their use, and the old patterns occur often in the *tragédies lyriques*. Sometimes they are slightly varied, and due to the simplicity of the descending line in the *chaconne* it is impossible to be certain that Lully himself was always conscious of his use of the bass patterns of the dances. It seems at times that his familiarity with the idiom may have caused him to use them unconsciously since he frequently begins a scene in this manner but makes no subsequent use of it.

In summary, the structure of scenes in the *tragédie lyrique* is based on recitative, and there are four main varieties: (1) recitative-dialogue without songs set in fixed forms; (2) recitative-dialogue containing songs and ending with an ensemble; (3) scene-complex; and (4) recitative-monologue. Within the context of these scenes, recitative is set in a similar manner. The organization of the poetry does not rule as the main determinant of musical setting; rather, what is set is the interpretation which would be given to that poetry by an actor. In many instances the poetry has been reorganized by the composer through repetition of lines in order to obtain semistructuring, thus enabling him to provide more variety in the musical setting. Melody, rhythm, and harmony are all used in such a way as to complement each other in bringing out the nuances and subtleties of meaning of the text. While formal musical structuring is not absent, musical settings are so conceived that the composer passes imperceptibly from freely through-composed sections into semistructured passages, thus gaining the variety necessary to make possible the use of long scenes in recitative.

NOTES

[1]Francois Raguenet, *A Comparison between the French and Italian Musick and Operas*, translator unknown (Farnborough: Gregg International Publishers, Ltd., 1968), pp. 5-7.

[2]Ibid., pp. 37-39.

[3]Raguenet, op. cit., p. 35, n. 22. He considers this to be a fault rather than a strength though he praises French recitative.

CHAPTER V

SUMMARY AND CONCLUSIONS

Lully's concept of musical drama for the French stage was the product of his own life and background. Though he was born in Italy, he came to France at the age of fourteen and participated in court life in the service of the cousin of the King until he was twenty. During this time he learned the art of the violinist and of the dancer for it was in these capacities that he entered the service of Louis XIV. Lully was soon appointed composer of instrumental music, and a few years later he was allowed to form a small orchestra to play music for the daily events of the King's life in spite of the opposition of the famed *Vingt-quatre violons du roi.* During his first years in the King's court Lully collaborated with others in writing *ballets de cour,* but bit by bit he became the sole composer just as Benserade became the sole poet. Molière and Lully then joined forces in the creation of the *comédie-ballet* for which Lully provided not only music for incidental songs but also composed entire scenes of dialogue. Lully also acted in the productions of the *comédies-ballets,* thus adding histrionic experience to the long list of skills on which he drew when finally he turned his attention to the creation of French opera.

When Lully obtained the patent for the academy and opera in 1672, he was already the most famous and most favored composer in France. The patent, however, gave him complete control over opera in that country, for he not only gained the right to support the enterprise through charging admission, but also performances of musical theater were made dependent on his approval; even the number of musicians who might be employed by other theaters was regulated. In addition to this he was given the right to form a school in which both vocal and instrumental musicians would be formed to perform operas. Lully supervised everything personally and set the manner in which both conservatories and opera houses have been managed ever since.

As for the *tragédie lyrique* itself, again Lully had complete control and was able to construct it entirely according to his own concepts. He rejected the use of pastorales as vehicles for musical theater, and once Quinault was placed under contract Lully remained loyal to his poet, though a court scandal forced him to make use of Thomas Corneille and his nephew Fontenelle as authors of two works. Machines and spectacular scenes were a feature of the *ballet de cour* as well as being the main characteristic of the popular machine plays. Lully assured their continued existence in his opera. He originally took the machinist, Carlo Vigarani, as his partner though later Lully assumed complete financial control and hired either Vigarani or Berain as machinist. After the writing of the opera, Lully became both dramatic coach and stage director so that no detail which might affect the quality of the production escaped his attention.

This form of organization gave a unity to the *tragédie lyrique* which was new to musical drama. Many of the poets and musicians who had previously taken part as collaborators in the *ballets de cour* and other court festivities made no secret of their displeasure, but Lully had secured the friendship of Louis XIV during the King's minority. *Tragédies lyriques*, in addition to gaining royal favor, drew huge audiences from all segments of French society. Contemporary journals attest to their immense popularity.

The manner in which the academy and opera were organized was based on the way in which Molière supported his theatrical troupe, a system which traces back to antiquity. This is in contrast to the production of court festivities and the *ballet de cour* wherein the court served as employer to a large number of authors and composers. The *tragédie lyrique* gained greatly from single leadership. In this multiple task, Lully made use of elements from all of the types of music and theatrical experience he had known, and he was successful both artistically and financially. This was due not only to his intelligence and talent but also to the fact that Lully chose to stress those factors which he knew would strike a responsive chord in the sophisticated audiences of late seventeenth-century France.

The *tragédie lyrique* was a combination of the various types of drama played in seventeenth-century France. Theater was the most widespread and the most popular French art form during the Baroque era. Over one thousand plays were performed both privately in various courts and publicly by the established companies of the Théâtre du Marais and the Hôtel de Bourgogne. Many works of literary criticism were written, and the formal structure of the genres became fixed. Music was employed in all types of drama excepting the classical tragedy.

French drama placed great emphasis on the development of two new elements in theater: the unities and linkage of scenes both of which affected the *tragédie lyrique*. The unities of time, place, and action caused playwrights to make their works concise. Unity of action was the most important in that observance of this rule tended to eliminate subplots and disconnected incidents thus focusing and intensifying the central intrigue throughout. Unity of place was not adopted in the *tragédie lyrique* because the operas depended in part on the use of machines, elaborate settings, and spectacles to charm the public. Unity of time was interpreted differently by various critics and authors, and was adopted in the *tragédie lyrique* only to the extent that the action requires the same time to perform on stage as would a similar incident in real life. The only exception is scenes in which spectacles take place.

Changes of scene in French drama depended on changes of actors on stage. A manner of moving smoothly from one scene to another was necessary, and the process of linkage through various means was devised. The most important of these was linkage of presence, that is, one or more characters should remain on stage to connect two scenes. Linkage was adopted in the *tragédie lyrique* and was further underscored by Lully because the continuo does not stop playing but rather uses the momentary pause between scenes to prepare the audience for the instrumental interludes which so often precede recitative-dialogue.

French theatrical practices were also influenced by Italian sixteenth-century theater. The unities were first formulated for Italian pastorales, and the authors and critics claimed to have taken the rules from Aristotle. Pastorales were cast in five acts with scene divisions and were given in sumptuous settings. They were enlivened by music, ballet, spectacular interludes, and lyrical choruses. Machines of marvelous construction were used, and Italian machinists were much in demand in France in the seventeenth-century. All of these elements are to be found in the *tragédie lyrique*, and Lully's partner was not his poet but his machinist, the Italian Carlo Vigarani. In addition to this, it is quite possible that French organization of theatrical troupes was based on that of the *commedia dell' arte*. The sets belonged to the entire company, and plays were given for public profit, while a single leader served both as chief actor and director of the productions.

The *tragédie lyrique*, as do Italian works, owes much to Seneca. His plays contained five acts, each of which terminated with a choral passage. They were based on Greek mythology, but Seneca altered the plots to conform to the taste of his day. He took it for granted that his audiences had a thorough acquaintance with the myths. He therefore was able to condense incidents and use references in order to advance action rather than having to portray each story in detail. As a Stoic philosopher, Seneca stressed the didactic element in his plays and presented the concept of virtue as a complement of self-restraint. All of these factors are also characteristic of the *tragédie lyrique.*

Aristotle's *Poetics* is the ultimate source from which the *tragédie lyrique* drew its origins. In this work the nature of theater is defined and the elements of its construction are discussed. Plot, character, thought, diction, music, and spectacle are placed in perspective, and the methods of handling them are set forth. Plot is restricted to a single action, the character of the protagonist is used to define various types of drama, appropriate means of expressing thought are treated, and the means of bringing about the denouement are measured and judged. Many modifications were made by subsequent critics and playwrights, but the basic concepts of theater were promulgated by Aristotle.

The large part given to recitative in the *tragédie lyrique* is caused by the dramatic form of the libretto. Not only does approximately half of each drama consist of recitative, but also four out of the five types of scene used in the *tragédie lyrique* depend on recitative for coherence. Recitative-dialogue scenes are of two types, those which contain many fixed forms and those which are mostly through-composed. The purpose of such scenes is to present an argument, a love scene, a discussion which clarifies an action which does not take place on stage, or to reveal character through contrast or comparison. Most of the *tragédies lyriques* begin with recitative-dialogue scenes; however, such scenes are used almost anywhere in an act, and there may be several of them occurring in succession. This type of scene is the most common in the *tragédie lyrique*.

Recitative-monologue scenes, while they are much rarer than recitative-dialogue, occupy key positions in the dramas in which they occur. They are sometimes used to introduce a drama, and in this way the protagonist is presented as is the case in *Atys*. More often, recitative-monologue occurs at a crucial point in the drama, and the subsequent action is changed by the scene.

Scene-complexes occur in each act and contain the spectacles which were adopted into the *tragédie lyrique* from the machine plays. While the main purpose of the scene-complex is centered in the spectacular element, nevertheless recitative plays an important role for it is through recitative that the action is explained. Scene-complexes are used for battles, weddings, sacrificial scenes, funeral scenes, and celebrations.

Within these large divisions, the musical setting of recitative is similar in organization and in the use of musical means to produce expressive interpretations of the text. The composer rather than the poet organized the text into structured and unstructured passages through repetition of lines in imitation of the procedure used in constructing *récits* in the *ballets de cour*. The poetry is cast in free verse, has an irregular meter, and the use of extended rhyme schemes tends both to link speeches and to cause a certain monotony. The text is lengthened and shortened by the composer through the use of different note-values and changing meters in order to approximate speech and indicate diction, thus enhancing the thoughts and emotions being expressed.

The melodies used in the setting of recitative range from *parlando* style, constructed mainly of triads and repeated notes, to arioso passages. Sometimes phrases are shaped so as to form arches or inverted arches. Scale passages, often quite extended, are used to increase dramatic tension. Skips are used both to set off individual words and to indicate a change of emotion. Melodic leaps of diminished fourths and fifths are used to portray anguish. Large downward leaps are used for the same purpose, while a sudden exclamation will be set with a large upward leap. The vocal range seldom exceeds an octave and a sixth and tends to be larger for the male voice than for the female. Settings are syllabic, and only rarely are two notes sung on a single syllable.

Rhythm is used with great subtlety and diversity from measure to measure, often as an important feature of textual expression. It is through the mixture of patterns, rests, driving sequences of notes of equal value, and contrasts of tempo that Lully achieves a musical setting which approximates speech. Sometimes rhythm is used to give a conversational tone to the text, sometimes to set off individual words, and sometimes Lully appears to desire straight-forward declamation without emotional emphasis being sought. The use of irregular lengths of phrases together with a consistent striving for variety helps to compensate for the overuse of the dactylic pattern. It should be noted that the changes of meter in the Lully recitative are not intended to produce the lilting rhythm found in Italian music. On the contrary, such changes accommodate the irregular lines of poetry, while at the same time they permit the composer to condense or lengthen a speech through changing note-values. Lully also indicates changes in tempo through meter signs.

Harmony is used both for musical variety and for expressive purposes. Each scene is set in a single basic key which is elaborated by short passages in a related key. Such transient modulations are used for the most part in order to give musical variety, but occasionally a third key center will be introduced at a dramatic or startling moment. Another harmonic device commonly use by Lully is the juxtaposition of a major triad with its parallel minor, producing glaring false relations. Such progressions are used to express a sudden change in feeling or an abrupt turn in the action. Harmonic rhythm generally underscores the quickening of speech as well as producing a drive toward cadences. Variety in Lully's recitative comes not so much from daring harmonic progressions as from the adroit use of melody and rhythm in which the text is set as it would be spoken.

Formal structuring within scenes based on recitative consists of two types: fixed forms and semistructured passages. The latter are by far the more common. The *récit* of the *ballet de cour* was the predecessor of the semistructured forms wherein composers often repeated the last line of poetry but set it with a different melody while retaining the rhythmic organization. Lully developed the manner of repeating lines of poetry with different melodies in order to obtain the semistructuring which gives variety to long scenes in recitative. Grounds also are used as structuring elements and are to be found throughout the *tragédies lyriques.* Structuring in scene-complexes is based on the media employed with exclamations by the chorus used in a *ritornello* fashion. Sometimes a *ritornello* design of this type is combined with the chaconne bass to create a mighty fresco as a final scene.

Recitative is accompanied by the continuo group with the exception of the recitative-monologue, which is accompanied by the full-orchestra. Even in scene-complexes, when a soloist sings in recitative style, the full orchestra does not play. Recitative-dialogue scenes are most often introduced by an instrumental piece marked *ritornello* invariably scored for two violins and continuo. The music of the *ritornello* does not return, and the two treble instruments drop out as the vocal part begins. When one of the characters in a recitative-dialogue scene is a bass, he very frequently will sing a semistructured or structured song which is scored for continuo and two treble instruments. The accompaniment of the recitative-monologue by the orchestra consists for the most part of a simple harmonization which allows the voice to stand out in relief. There are frequent orchestral interludes which give variety of timbre.

Although ten of the thirteen *tragédies lyriques* are based on stories from Greek and Roman mythology and the other three on legendary French heroes, Quinault transformed each subject so that the French aristocratic concepts of love and glory were portrayed. According to this ideal, the true hero was motivated by magnanimity to perform great acts of heroism and was rewarded through the intervention of supernatural beings by attaining union in perfect love with an ideal heroine. The difference between ideal love and mere passion is demonstrated through the reaction of the hero or heroine to jealousy, for the noble soul who is not able to win the object of his affections must renounce his claim and follow glory. The baser soul seeks vengeance. Ambition and vanity are condemned, for protagonists who succumb to such motivation are punished by downfall. These ideals are not unique to Quinault but on the contrary, are to be found in much French literature of the early seventeenth century, especially in the works of Pierre Corneille.

Given the importance of the expression of this concept, delineation of character is vital to the *tragédie lyrique.* Quinault proceeds in a variety of ways. The protagonist who is noble always acts and speaks in a manner consistent with his glory. Often there are contrasting characters who underscore his nobility by their base reactions to similar situations and emotions. The protagonist is seen through the eyes of all the subordinate characters who express their opinions of him, and in the final act of each opera his triumph or downfall is brought about by the gods or by magical means. Frequent maxims are spoken by secondary characters in further commentary on the character of the protagonist. As a poet, Quinault had his faults, but character delineation was one of his great strengths.

Strong dramatic progression is another characteristic of the *tragédie lyrique*. Quinault had written spoken tragedy before becoming the poet of the opera, and he followed the basic rules of French classical drama. The entire libretto of an opera consists of a series of dramatic incidents carefully chosen to proceed with mounting tension toward a climax. Further, each act follows a similar plan. At the same time, the conditions are set for the next act through logical progression of events or by some twist in plot. Main characters are introduced in the first act and the action is outlined. Conflict appears in the second act, while in the third act it becomes evident that the conflict must be resolved. The fourth act contains the denouement, and in the fifth act the protagonist is either rewarded or his downfall is brought about. The same basic plan serves for all *tragédies lyriques*.

Given the strength of the dramatic element and of the text, the musical setting of Quinault's plays had to be different from the settings of the plots of Italian opera. Since Lully called the works *tragédies lyriques* and did not hesitate to manipulate the text both before and after its approval by the French Academy, it is certain that he thought the drama to be at least equally important with the music. Lully invented the French recitative with the purpose of stressing the drama and the text, and it is for this reason that recitative dominates and becomes, in fact, the greatest single controlling element in establishing those characteristics which for centuries distinguish French opera from that of any other land.

In summary, the *tragédies lyriques* by Quinault and Lully were products of a long line of theatrical works dating back to antiquity. Their structure was drawn from French tragedy, machine plays, *ballet de cour, comédie-ballet,* and Italian opera, and all combined to create a form in which drama, music, and spectacle receive almost equal stress--in a form and style unique to France. The nature of the drama is such that long scenes of recitative are necessary to promote dramatic progression and the delineation of character. Lully invented a style of recitative for this purpose which moves freely from *parlando* to *arioso* and back to *parlando*; a procedure by means of which he was able to throw into sharp relief the events and emotions portrayed in the text. While the use of melody, rhythm, and harmony in the Lully recitative are similar throughout the operas, he set five basic types of scene, four of which are dependent on recitative though semistructuring fixed forms occur.

The form given to the *tragédie lyrique* by Lully was the product of his experience as a musician and an actor, and he assured the quality of the performances by his influence at court and by supervising every detail of each performance personally. This form was so well suited to French taste that the main characteristics of the *tragédie lyrique* became those of French opera throughout its history.

APPENDIX I

LISTING OF THE TRAGEDIES LYRIQUES

In the following listing of the *tragédies lyriques* the name of the librettist is given, together with the dates of the first performance for the King and court, the last public performance, and the history of the printings by the firm, Christophe Ballard. Some works were not originally produced for the King; such premieres took place in Paris at the Théâtre de l'Académie (Palais-Royal).

Cadmus et Hermione, Quinault, Saint-Germain, April 27, 1673; last performance, 1737; edition, 1720.

Alceste, Quinault, Saint-Germain, January 6, 1674; repeated until 1757; editions, 1708, 1727, 1757.

Thésée, Quinault, Saint-Germain, January 11, 1675; Paris, April, 1675; repeated as written until 1779, and with revisions by Gossec in 1782; editions, 1688, 1711, 1720.

Atys, Quinault, Saint-Germain, January 10, 1676; Paris, April, 1676; repeated until 1740; editions, 1689, 1708, 1715, 1720.

Isis, Quinault, Saint-Germain, January 5, 1677; Paris, April, 1677; repeated until 1732; editions, 1699, 1719.

Psyché, Thomas Corneille and Fontenelle, Paris, April 19, 1678; repeated until 1713; edition, 1720.

Bellérophon, Thomas Corneille and Fontenelle, Paris, January 31, 1679; repeated until 1728; editions, 1679, 1714.

Proserpine, Quinault, Saint-Germain, February 3, 1680; Paris, November 15, 1680; repeated until 1758; editions, 1680, 1707, 1714.

Persée, Quinault, Paris, April 18, 1682; repeated until 1746; editions, 1682, 1710, 1722.

Phaéton, Quinault, Versailles, January 6, 1683; Paris, April 27, 1683; repeated until 1742; editions, 1683, 1709, 1711, 1721.

Amadis, Quinault, Paris, January 18, 1684; repeated until 1771; editions, 1684, 1711, 1719, 1759.

Roland, Quinault, Versailles, January 18, 1685; Paris, March 8, 1685; repeated until 1755; editions, 1685, 1709, 1716.

Armide, Quinault, Paris, February 15, 1686; repeated until 1764 as written, with revisions by Francoeur, 1781; editions, 1686, 1710, 1725.

APPENDIX II

LETTRE PATENTE

Text of the *Lettre Patente* given to Lully for the establishment of the opera and the *Académie Royale.*

Louis, etc.--. Les sciences et les arts estant les ornemens les plus considérables des Estats, nous n'avons point eu de plus agréables divertissements, depuis que nous avons donné las paix à nos peuples, que de les faire revivre en appelant auprès de nous tous ceux qui se sont acquis la réputation d'y exceller, non-seulement dans l'estendue de nostre royaume, mais aussy dans les plays estrangers; et pour les obliger davantage à s'y perfectionner, nous les avons honorés des marques de nostre estime et de nostre bienveillance. Et comme entre les arts libéraux la musique y tient un des premiers rangs, nous aurions, dans le dessein de la faire réussir avec tous ses avantages, par nos lettres patentes du 28 juin 1669, accordé au sieur Perrin la persmission d'establir en nostre bonne ville de Paris et autres de nostre royaume des académies de musique pour chanter en public des pièces de théâtre, comme il se pratique en Italie, en Allemagne at en Angleterre, pendant l'éspace de douze années. Mais ayant esté depuis informé que les peines et les soins que le sieur Perrin a pris pour cet establissement n'ont pu seconder pleinement nostre intention et élèver la musique au point que nous nous l'estions promis, nous avons cru que pour y mieux réussir il estoit à propos d'en donner la conduite à une personne don't l'éxpérience et la capacité nous fussent connues et qui eust assez de suffisance, tant pour former des élèves pour bein chanter et actionner sur le théâtre qu'à dresser des bandes de violons, flustes et autres instrumens.
A ces causes, bien informé de l'intelligence et grande connoissances que s'est acquise nostre cher et bienamé Jean-Baptiste Lully au fait de la musique, dont il nous a donné et donne journellement de très-agréables preuves, depuis plusiers années qu'il s'est attaché à nostre service, qui nous ont convié de l'honorer de la charge de surintendant et compositeur de la musique de nostre chambre; nous avons audit sieur Lully permis et accordé, permettons et accordons par ces présentes signées de nostre main, d'establir une académie royale de musique dans nostre bonne ville de Paris, qui sera composée de tel nombre et quantité de personnes qu'il avisera bonestre, que nous arresterons et choisirons sur le rapport qu'il nous en fera, pour faire des représentations devant nous, quand il nous plaira, des pièces de musique qui seront composées tant en vers français qu'autres langues estrangères, pareille et semblable aux académies d'Italie, pour en jouir sa vie durant,

et après luy celuy de ses enfans qui sera pourvu et reçu en survivance de ladite charge de surintendant de la musique de nostre chambre, avec pouvoir d'associer avec luy qui bon luy semblera pour l'establissement de ladite académie. Et pour dédommager des grands frais qu'il conviendra faire pour lesdites représentations, tant à cause des théâtres, machines, décorations, habits, qu'autres choses necessaires, nous luy permettons de donner au public toutes les pièces qu'il aura composées, mesme celles qui auront esté représentées devant nous, sans néanmoins qu'il puisse se servir, pour l'éxécution desdites pièces, des musiciens qui sont à nos gages; comme aussy de prendre telles sommes qu'il jugera à propos et d'establir des gardes et autres gens necessaires aux portes des lieux où se feront lesdites représentations; faisant très-expresses inhibitions et défenses à toutes personnes de quelque qualité et condition qu'elles soyent, mesme aux officiers de nostre maison, d'y entrer sans payer; comme aussy de faire chanter aucune pièce entière en musique, soit en françois ou autre langue, sans la permission par écrit du sieur Lully, à peine de 10,000 livres d'amende et de confiscaton des théâtres, machines, décorations, habits et autres choses, applicables, un tiers à noùs, un tiers à l'hôpital general et l'autre tiers audit sieur Lully, lequel pourra aussy establir des écôles particulières de musique dans nostre bonne ville de Paris et partout où il jugera necessaire pour le bien et avantage de ladite académie royale. Et d'autant que nous l'érigeons sur le pied des académies d'Italie, où les gentils-hommes chantent publiquement en musique sans déroger, voulons et nous plaist que tous gentilhommes et damoiselles puissent chanter audites pièces et représentations de nostre académie royale, sans que pour ce ils soyent censés déroger audit titre de noblesse et à leur priviléges, charges, droits et immunités.

Revoquons, cassons, et annulons par ces présentes toutes permissions et priviléges que nous pourrions avoir cy-devant donnés et accordés, mesme celuy dudit Perrin, pour raison desdites pièces de théâtre en musique, sous quelque nom, qualité, condition et prétexte que ce puisse estre.

LOUIS

COLBERT

From: *Lettres, Instructions, et mémoires de Colbert,* Vol. V, edited by Pierre Clément. Paris: Imprimerie impériale, 1868, pp. 535-36.

APPENDIX III

SYNOPSIS AND DERIVATION OF PLOTS

Cadmus et Hermione is discussed at length in Chapter III, pages 69-71.

Alceste

The prologue of *Alceste* is an allegory in which the nymphes of the Seine and the Marne dispute the favor of the unnamed hero. The nymph of the Seine loves him and awaits his return from the wars. She is told that she will not find her hero without glory.

Alceste is roughly based on the play by Euripides rather than on the ancient myth and was called a prosatyric play rather than a tragedy by Gilbert Murray.[1] Alceste was the most beautiful daughter of Pelias, and Admetus, King of Pherae, sought the help of Apollo to win her. The couple omitted the customary sacrifices to Artemis who replaced Alcestis with a nest of serpents. Apollo again intervened, and Artemis gave the promise that on his day of death, Admetus would be spared on the condition that a member of his family would die for him out of love. Hermes arrived one morning, far sooner than anyone expected, to summon Admetus to Tartarus. Apollo again intervened and gained some time by getting the Three Fates drunk. This is the point at which the play begins. Admetus, after being refused by everyone else, has prevailed upon Alcestis to take his place, an act she is willing to do more for love of her children and concern for their fate than for Admetus. She begs him to swear that he will not remarry, which he does while feeling terribly sorry for himself that he must lose his dear wife. Meanwhile, Hercules (Herakles, or Alcides) has come to the house as a guest, and Admetus has given orders that he is to be well received and not told of the sorrow of the household. Hercules gets drunk and abuses one of the servants who tells him the truth. The demigod then offers to go to the underworld to rescue Alcestis, and all ends happily. Quinault's transformation of the plot of Alceste has been discussed on pages 71-72.

Thésée

The prologue of Thésée is set at Versailles. Venus and Mars, symbolizing love and glory, have come to celebrate the fame of the world's greatest hero.

The main drama is based on the early life of Thésée. Aegeus, the Father of Theseus, had no children by his first two wives. On a voyage home from the Delphic oracle which he had consulted about his childlessness, Aegeus stopped at Troezen to visit his old friends, Pittheus and Troezen. Pittheus' daughter, Aethra, had been engaged to Bellérophon before he had been exiled but now, though still contracted to him, she had little hope of marriage. Her father, influenced by a spell cast by Medea, caused her to lie with Aegeus. The same night she lay with Neptune, but a bargain was made that any child born would be considered to belong to Aegeus. Aegeus, when he awoke, told Aethra that if a son were born to her she should rear him secretly at Troezen. He then hid his sword and his sandals under a hollow rock and told Aethra that when their son grew up, if he was able to move the rock and recover the tokens, she should send him with them to Athens. In due time, Theseus was born, grew to young manhood, lifted the rock, and went to his father having many heroic adventures on the way. Aegeus, meanwhile, had honored his promise to Medea and given her refuge, though he did not know that Aethra had borne him a son, and Medea, also, had conceived by Aegeus. She recognized Theseus at once and planned to secure his death by having his own father, Aegeus, poison him. At the last moment, Aegeus recognized his sword and dashed the wine to the ground. Medea escaped, and the Athenians rejoiced with Theseus.

In the Quinault version, Aeglé, one of the maidens sent to King Minos for sacrifice to the minotaur, is in Athens. She loves Thésée, and he loves her. Aegée is betrothed to Médée, but he also loves Aeglé, while Médée is enamored of Thésée whose identity she knows. Médée draws Thésée into telling her of his love for Aeglé and promises to help him win her. She then menaces Aeglé saying that if the latter will not pretend that she no longer loves Thésée and now wishes to marry Aegée, Médée will kill Thésée.

Thésée is so afflicted by Aeglé's false statement that he bursts into tears, and Thésée forces her to tell him the truth. Their vows of eternal faith and love are overheard by Médée who promises that she will help them. Thésée has proven himself to be an able warrior in the defense of Athens, and Aegée is preparing to recognize him as his heir in the victory celebration. Médée convinces Aegée that Thésée is a menace to him because of Thésée's great popularity with the people. She also reminds him that he has a son who would be disinherited if Thésée becomes Aegée's heir.

Aegée is troubled; however, under Médée's influence, he consents to kill Thésée. Médée is jubilant for nothing less than filial murder will calm her feelings of jealousy. In the midst of the celebration Thésée draws his sword to swear allegiance to Aegée who recognizes it as his own. Médée knows that her plan has failed and escapes in her winged chariot calling forth all her evil power to destroy everything behind her. Minerve intervenes and saves the city after which the marriage of Thésée and Aeglé is celebrated with great rejoicing by the people of Athens.

Atys

The prologue of *Atys* contains a reference to the coming drama. Le Temps is holding a festival to celebrate the fame of the greatest of heroes in all history. Cybelle interrupts the festivities and proposes to bring to life the story of Atys for the entertainment of the great new hero.

Cybelle was a Phrygian goddess, often identified with Rhea, wife of Cronus and mother of Hestia, Pluto, Poseidon, Zeus, Hera, and Demeter. She fell in love with the mortal, Atys, but he scorned her. In vengence, she castrated him, and he bled to death. A widespread cult developed in the Near East in which the followers of Cybelle attempted to achieve ecstatic union with the goddess through self-castration and dressing themselves like women.[2]

In Quinault's transformation, Cybelle comes to earth to live for love of Atys. Atys loves Sangaride who is betrothed to the King, Celanus. Cybelle chooses Atys to be her high priest making it clear that what she desires is not honor, but love. Celanus says he will console himself by marrying Sangaride. Cybelle, questioned by her servant, confesses that she is victim of a passion so great that she has renounced her own glory to be near the object of her affection. Atys and Sangaride decide that their love is hopeless and that they should follow the path of honor and duty, but as Sangaride's marriage approaches she becomes quite desperate and wishes to throw herself on Cybelle's mercy, to be released from her betrothal. Atys is at first shocked that Sangaride could treat her vows of faith to Celanus so lightly, but his love is so strong that it overcomes his sense of honor. He falls asleep and in his slumber dreams of the sweetness of honor and glory. Morphée tells him:

Mais souviens-toy que la beauté
Quand elle est Imortelle
Demande la fidélité
D'une amour éternelle.[3]

Terrifying dreams then come to plague him, and he is told that unless he is faithful to Cybelle he will die. The goddess is there as he awakens and assures him that she sent the dreams and that they are true.

Atys and Sangaride nevertheless ask Cybelle to prevent the marriage of Sangaride and Celanus. The goddess understands their feelings, but she allows the drama to play itself out. She laments her own fate, to have given up heaven, honor, glory, and position for a man who does not care for her. Cybelle persuades Celanus to aid her in obtaining vengeance. He organizes a celebration at which Atys presides as high priest. Cybelle makes Atys imagine that he sees a monster which he kills with his sword in honor of the goddess. She brings him to his senses, and Atys sees that it is his beloved Sangaride whom he has murdered. Celanus is horrified at such a terrible vengeance, and Cybelle herself relents only to find that Atys has taken his own life. She cannot follow him because she is immortal so she transforms him into a tree which she will always love.

Atys is the first tragédie lyrique to have a tragic ending. In it Quinault shows how actions which are not in accord with the noble ideal will bring defeat and punishment. Not only is love in opposition to glory in this opera, but also it is shown that if love is placed more highly than honor, it will bring unhappiness even to one of the immortals. All three of the main characters place love first in their lives. Sangaride refuses to keep her given word because of it. Atys betrays Cybelle through both jealousy and love. Cybelle gives up her position and honor for a love which she knows is unworthy of her.

Isis

The prologue of Isis is a festival celebrating the pleasures of joy and song instead of war. There are no references to the coming drama.

Isis is based on the story of the nymph, Io. Jupiter fell in love with Io, and in order to fulfill his passion he enveloped the two of them in a dark cloud hoping in this way to escape detection by Juno. The queen of the gods, however, noticing this unnatural phenomenon, immediately suspected that her husband was up to some kind of trick and ordered the cloud to dissipate. There stood Jupiter, and beside him was a beautiful heifer. Juno did not believe his lie that the creature had just sprung up from earth and asked to have the little animal as a gift. Jupiter could not refuse, and Juno placed Io under the guard of Argus. Jupiter called on Mercury to put Argus to sleep and kill him which Mercury accomplished by telling the story of Pan and Syrinx. Io should have been free then, but Junon sent a gad-fly to sting her into madness driving her from country to country. The Ionian sea is named for her, as is the Bosphorus, or Ford of the Cow. At last she reached the Nile after years of wandering, and there Zeus restored her to human form. She bore him a son, Epaphus, and afterwards lived forever, happy and honored.

In the Quinault version, Io is engaged to Hierax when Jupiter comes to woo her. Mercure warns his master of Junon's approach and Jupiter asks Mercure to detain Iris, Junon's messenger, while he makes his escape. In the scene which follows Quinault cleverly portrays the nature of true love by contrasting it with false declaration.

Mercure can find no better way to delay Iris than by telling her he wishes to talk with her only because he loves her. Iris tells Mercure that it is fun to listen to such a declaration but that it isn't very believable. He swears to serve her and her alone, in spite of his arduous duties to Jupiter. She, in turn, tells him that all of her life she has desired to find a true and faithful lover. They swear to love each other eternally, never hiding anything from one another, living in complete confidence forever. Iris' first question is why did Jupiter come down to earth? Mercure answers that it was for the good of all mankind. Iris contradicts him saying that she was hiding behind a cloud and saw Jupiter flirting with that nymph. Mercure accuses her of lack of candor, and Iris accuses him of lying. The scene ends with a duo in which they swear to take their hearts back eternally and to love no more.

Junon, in jealousy, asks Jupiter for a new handmaiden in such a way that he cannot refuse. He is shocked when she asks for Io whom she places under the guard of Argus. Mercure tries to make Argus close all of his hundred eyes by staging a festival based on the story of Pan and Syrinx. Io is on the point of escaping when Hierax, her former fiancé, awakens Argus who calls Junon. The goddess sends Io to the ends of the earth pursued by the furies until the nymph wishes only for death. Jupiter upbraids Junon and asks her if she is so inhuman that she has no pity at all, and Junon answers by asking him if he, the greatest of all the gods, is unable to master his own emotions. They promise each other to change their ways and learn better conduct. Io is elevated to the status of an immortal under the name of Isis and is invited by Junon to enjoy eternal happiness.

Psyché

The first libretto produced by Corneille and Fontenelle was a re-working of the machine play, *Psyché*, written in 1671 in collaboration by Molière, Pierre Corneille, and Quinault. Louis XIV was so fond of the music from this work that he asked Lully to arrange it for the celebration of the siege and investment of Dunquerque.[4]

The prologue is an allegory about the ending of wars.
The time for peace and for love have come. There is no reference to
the coming drama.

The story of Psyché is told only by Apuleius in the second
century A.D. Psyché was a mortal, youngest of three princesses and the
most beautiful. Everyone who saw her was so captivated by her
loveliness that men deserted the alters of the goddess Venus. In anger,
Venus ordered her son, Cupid, to seek out Psyché and afflict her with a
passion for an ugly and horrible monster--but she allowed Cupid to see
Psyché first that he might recognize her. Cupid fell in love with Psyché,
and, instead of making her fall in love, he saw to it that though all
should admire her none could love her. Psyché's two sisters were
splendidly married, but Psyché sat day after day, alone and neglected.
At last her father went to consult an oracle of Apollo. The oracle,
having been instructed by Cupid, told the King to expose his daughter
on a hill, dressed in mourning, alone, and there her chosen husband, a
terrible serpent, would come and fetch her. Psyché, in despair, consented
but instead of a serpent, gentle winds came to get her and they put her
down near a pleasant stream where she fell asleep. She awakened to
find a lovely mansion close by and voices whispering in her ears told her
to enter and make this her home. That night, Cupid came to her in
darkness, and Psyché's joy was almost boundless. Almost, because after a
time she began to miss her family, and when Cupid told her that her
sisters were approaching and that she must not see them, she burst into
tears and begged him to allow her to meet them. They, in jealousy of
her good fortune, convinced her that she was really the bride of a
monster and that she must try to see him and kill him in his sleep.
Psyché was persuaded, but as she tried to follow her sisters' advice, the
lamp she carried dripped hot oil on Cupid, injuring him. He jumped up
and fled, and the palace disappeared, while Psyché was left with the
realization that her own lack of faith in what she knew to be true had
brought about her unhappiness. She wandered from country to country
trying to find Cupid without success and at last determined to consult
Venus. Venus set her to accomplish four impossible tasks, the last of
which was to procure a boxful of Proserpine's beauty. Knowing that her
travels and suffering had impaired her own beauty, Psyché opened the
box and fell into a deep sleep. Meanwhile, Venus had used the pretext of
healing Cupid's wound to lock him in his room, but the wound had
healed, he longed for Psyché, and he flew out the window to find her.
He wiped the sleep from her eyes and put it back in the box and
awakened her with a prick from one of his arrows and sent her to his
mother, telling her all would be well. Cupid appealed to Jupiter, who as
all know could never resist the power of Cupid, and Jupiter called

together all of the gods and goddesses. He told them of the marriage of Cupid and Psyché and announced that as a wedding gift he would bestow immortality on the bride. Venus could no longer object to having Psyché as a daughter-in-law and peace returned to Olympus. As stated in Chapter III, the myth of Psyché is followed quite closely in the *tragédie lyrique*; however, Venus has been substituted for Psyché's sister as the agent who tempts the heroine.

Bellérophon

The prologue of *Bellérophon* is set on Mount Parnassus. Apollon and the Muses, Bacchus, Pan, troupes of shepherds and shepherdesses, and Egyptians are all gathered to sing praises to the hero of France. There is no reference to the coming drama.

The story of Bellérophon is very old for some of the incidents in it were told by Hesiod. Most of the story was told by Pindarus in the first half of the fifth century B.C. Only a portion of the story is used in the *tragédie lyrique*. Bellérophon was assumed to be the son of Glaucus, King of Ephyre (Corinth). Actually, he was the son of Neptune, and this explains the favor shown to him by the gods. Athena had taught his mother, and the goddess extended her protection to the son and helped him to catch Pegasus, the winged horse. Accidentally, Bellérophon killed his brother and went to Argos where he was purified by King Proteus. This previous knowledge of the story is assumed by Corneille and Fontenelle. As Bellérophon continued to perform great deeds, the wife of Proteus, Anteia, fell in love with him, and when he repudiated her advances, she told Proteus that their guest, Bellérophon, had wronged her and that he must die. Proteus could not kill Bellérophon, however, because of the deep traditions of hospitality and, instead, he sent the youth to take a letter to the King of Lycia. The Lycians entertained Bellérophon for several days before opening the letter which said that Proteus wanted the young man killed, but the same laws of hospitality which restrained the hand of Proteus now restrained the Lycians. The King, thinking to fulfill Proteus' wishes, sent Bellérophon to kill the Chimera--lion, goat and serpent at once--but with the aid of Pegasus, this was no great task to Bellérophon. After numerous other hazardous labors, Bellérophon won Proteus over and was married to his daughter. For the discussion of Quinault's version of Bellérophon, see pages 74-75.

Proserpine

The prologue of *Proserpine* is an allegorical dispute between La Discorde and La Victoire. La Discorde holds as prisoners la Paix, la

Felicité, l'Abondance, les Jeux, and les Plaisirs.   La Victoire, always
on the side of justice, fights Discorde and frees them all.

The story of Demeter and Proserpine is very old and has been
told in a great number of versions with varying details. Quinault appears
to have drawn on a number of these.   With the exception of a few
details and taking into account the foreshortening necessary for theatrical
reasons, Quinault left the myth very much in its original form.

Ceres, goddess of the earth, loves her daughter by Jupiter more
than anything on earth, and Proserpine is happy with her mother.
Jupiter sends Mercure to earth to bid Ceres to visit him, and previous
knowledge of the plot causes the audience to be aware that Jupiter does
not dare to actually approve of the marriage of Proserpine for fear of
offending Ceres.   Ceres charges her servant, the nymph Arethuse, to
guard her beloved daughter during her absence.   Alphée loves Arethuse,
and in the concern of the latter with her own love, she allows Pluton to
hide in the bushes so that he can watch Proserpine gather flowers with
the other nymphes.   Pluton seizes Proserpine and carries her off to the
underworld. The nymphes search everywhere but Proserpine is nowhere
to be found.   At last Arethuse decides to make the voyage to the
underworld and Alphée accompanies her for: "Le bonheur est partout
où l'Amour est en paix."[5]

When Ceres returns and finds her daughter gone, she is
distraught and feels keenly the injustice that she, who brings abundance
to the earth, should be punished in this way. She decides that she will
withhold her gifts and cease making the earth blossom until her daughter
is found.

Meanwhile, Pluton is vainly trying to win Proserpine's love. She
wishes to return to her mother but was tempted into eating by Ascalphe,
whom she turns into an owl. This detail is transformed, for in the myth
Ascalphe merely tells Hades that Proserpine/Core has eaten seven
pomegranate seeds.   Demeter/Ceres finding out that Ascalphe is
responsible for her loss of Proserpine for four/six/seven months of the
year changes him into an owl after Hercules released Ascalphe from the
hole she had pushed him into and covered with a rock.   Previous
knowledge on the part of the audience is again assumed for no mention
is made of the pomegranate seeds, merely of Proserpine's having eaten.
Pluton calls upon the Shades to help him woo Proserpine and they sing
to her:

Rien n'est impossible à l'Amour constant.[6]

Qu'il est doux d'avoir charmé
Un coeur qui n'a jamais aimé.[7]

Proserpine longs for her mother and the beauties of the earth but Pluton, though he is ever kind, loving, and patient, tells her that he will continue to love her even though she resists him forever.

The destruction wreaked on earth by Ceres' neglect is so great that Jupiter decides to make Pluton give up Proserpine. The Shades refuse to let their Queen go, and as the forces of heaven and the underworld prepare to do battle Ceres learns that her daughter reigns over the realm of darkness. The compromise of having Proserpine spend several months of each year with her mother and the rest of the year with Pluton is effectuated by Mercure--this is not explained to the audience--and all take part in the magnificent wedding of Pluton and Proserpine. In the myth Jupiter sends his mother, Rhea, to plead with Ceres to return to Olympus and fulfill her calling on earth once more, and it is Rhea, mother of Ceres and Pluton as well as of Jupiter, who negotiates the compromise.

Persée

The prologue of *Persée* is an allegory in which la Vertu and la Fortune swear that they will always serve the greatest of all heroes, the one who has brought peace to the whole earth.

Some of the incidents in *Persée* are based on the Greek myth. If the basic action is considered to be the love of Persée and Andromède, then the acts of heroism which result in their final union become part of the single action. It is obvious that the acts of heroism were of primary importance to the Greeks and these, rather than the story of Andromède, Merope, and Persée are what has been adapted from the original myth. Persée was the son of Danae who had been locked up by her father as the result of a prophesy that Acrisius would be killed by his grandson. Zeus visited her, and when Persée was born, Acrisius placed the mother and child in a chest which floated across the sea to the island Seriphon. The King of that island wished to marry Danae, and in a plot to rid himself of Persée the King demanded that the young man bring him the head of Medusa. Medusa, the mortal member of the trio of Gorgons, had once been very beautiful, but she offended Athena and in punishment (for acting like a scatter-brained flighty girl and profaning the temple of Athena) the goddess transformed one side of her head so that the very sight of the golden locks turned into snakes would turn a man to stone. Athena became the protectress of Persée and arranged for him to acquire her shield, Hermes' sickle, winged sandals, a magic wallet to contain the head, and Pluton's helmet of invisibility. Persée found the Gorgons asleep, and with Athena to guide his arm he cut off Medusa's head with a single stroke of the sickle. To his surprise, Pegasus and the warrior Chrysaor sprang fully grown from her body. They awakened the other two Gorgons, but Persée made his escape by donning Pluton's helmet and flying off with his winged sandals. On his journey homeward he had various adventures and dropped some of Medusa's blood on the desert where a swarm of venomous serpents arose. As he rounded the coast of Philistia, he saw a beautiful naked woman chained to a rock and fell in love with her. It was Andromède, daughter of Cepheus, King of Joppa, and of Cassiopeia. Due to Cassiopeia's boasting of her own and her daughter's beauty Neptune had demanded this sacrifice to placate the Nereids who were under his protection. Persée exacted the promise from Cepheus and Cassiopeia that if he were able to rescue Andromède, he would become her husband. At the celebration of the wedding, however, Agenor arrived with a party of armed men to claim Andromède for himself. Cepheus and Cassiopeia claimed that this King had a prior claim to Andromède. Persée gave battle but was seriously outnumbered so he withdrew the head of Medusa from the magic wallet and turned his enemies to stone. He had further adventures before arriving in his homeland and accidentally killing his grandfather, but his marriage with Andromède is the culminating point of the *tragédie lyrique*.

Two new characters have been introduced in the story by Quinault: Phinée and Merope. Phinée was actually Agenor's son and as for Merope, she was one of the Pleiads, in no way related to the story of Persée. Andromède is present from the beginning of the drama.

Merope and Cassiope reveal that Meduse is being inspired by Junon to terrify all of the inhabitants of the land and if nothing is done, the country will soon be peopled by inanimate rocks. Merope loves Persée, but he loves Andromède who is betrothed to Phinée. Persée says he will fight Meduse if he can marry Andromède. The gods favor Persée, and Mercure brings him Vulcan's sword, the shield of Pallas, and the helmet of Pluton. Merope is so moved by the thought of danger to Persée that she agrees to join forces with Andromède to help him, while Phinée hopes that Persée will perish and that he will still be able to marry Andromède.

Mercure helps Persée by making the Gorgons fall asleep and Persée kills Meduse. The other two Gorgons, awakening, tell Persée he will now die for a monster is rising from each drop of Meduse's blood. Mercure tells Persée to flee and opens a great hole in the ground which swallows up the monsters and the Gorgons.

Merope and Phinée decide to unite themselves in gaining vengeance on Persée and Andromède out of jealousy, but Merope is horrified to discover that Phinée would rather see Andromède dead than happy in the arms of another. Junon has sent a monster to devour Andromède, but Persée does battle with it and is once again victorious.

Phinée tells Merope that he will lead warriors against Persée and since he has the favor of Junon, he will succeed in defeating the great hero. Merope cannot betray her love and reveals to Persée that Phinée is coming to attack him. The battle is almost lost when Persée arrives with the head of Meduse, and the entire army of the enemy is turned to stone. The opera ends with the chorus singing that nothing can be sweeter than love and glory together.

Phaéton

> The prologue of *Phaéton* consists of a festival of the gods and goddesses to entertain the great new hero who is presently living with the mortals. There is no reference to the coming drama.

The myth of Phaéton has been altered in order to stress the ambitious side of the nature of the protagonist. Phaéton was the son of Rhode and Helius. (She was also known by the names of both of her daughters, Prote and Clymène.) He persuaded his father to allow him to drive his chariot, the Sun, across the skies for one day in order to show off in front of his sisters. Phaéton drove the horses first too high and the earth shivered, then too low and it was scorched. Zeus, in anger, killed him with a thunderbolt and Phaéton fell into the River Po. In Ovid's re-telling of the tale, many incidents were added. Rather than his sisters, Phaéton wished to impress his school friends who would not believe that his father was a god. Helius then swears to grant Phaéton any wish by the River Styx at which the rash youth demands to conduct the Sun for one day. Helius warns him that he is part mortal and that the horses which draw the chariot are very wild and fierce, but nothing will deter the boy. The horses become uncontrollable as Phaéton tires, and the gods and goddesses beg Jupiter to put end to the destruction which he does by killing Phaéton with a thunderbolt and bringing the chariot to earth.

Quinault has added some characters, Libye, Epaphus, and Théone, whom he has used without the slightest regard for their identities. Epaphus was the son of Io and Jupiter. Libye was his daughter and bore Agenor and Belus, twins, to Poseidon. Théone is a name borrowed from the *Iliad*. She was the daughter of Thestor and sister of Calchas. Quinault uses these three to create the love quadrangle: Phaéton is loved by Libye but out of ambition wishes to marry Théone who loves and is loved by Epaphus.

As the opera opens, Libye speaks of her past happiness. She and Phaéton were in love, but now his character has changed and she fears for the future. Phaéton tells her she is exaggerating, but in an interview with his mother, Clymène, the Queen, he shows that Libye is right. Phaéton is now motivated only by conceit and ambition. He fears that Epaphus, the son of Jupiter, will be chosen as heir to the throne, and, even though he must give up Libye and marry Théone, the King's daughter, Phaéton asks Clymène to intervene with her husband the King in his favor. Clymène fears evil omens and goes to consult Protée. Triton helps her to capture Protée and, after the latter changes himself into the shapes of many animals, he at last reveals that Phaéton is doomed unless he renounces his ambition. Phaéton refuses to accept the prophecy and Clymène, against her will, agrees to persuade the King to grant Phaéton's wish.

When Phaéton goes to the temple of Isis to make the required sacrifice he meets Epaphus who taunts him with the fact that no one knows who Phaéton's father is. After all, it is only Clymène's word that he is the son of Helius. Phaéton is further angered when Isis closes the temple doors and refuses to accept his sacrifice. He seeks out Helius and implores him to show his favor. Helius consents and assures Phaéton that he is truly his son. From here to the end, the *tragédie lyrique* is faithful to Ovid's version of the myth. The final words of the opera are a condemnation of Phaéton's ambition and temerity.

Amadis

Quinault has drawn on the first four books of the medieval romance, *Amadis de Gaule*, for the characters and incidents which he freely wove into the story of the *tragédie lyrique*. A retelling of the original would have been both impossible and undesirable. The romance is cast in the medieval form wherein many characters and stories run continuously in and out around a central theme. To project such a story on stage was impossible without returning to the medieval dramatic forms such as the *Mystère*. Quinault seriously reduced the number of characters retaining only two pair of lovers, two pair of magicians, their servants, and a ghost from the two hundred fifty-eight which were counted by Grace A. Williams in her study.[8] To trace the origin of each character and incident used by Quinault in the present work would require a great number of pages; therefore, only the story of the *tragédie lyrique* will be told below.

The prologue to *Amadis* is sung by the magicians Urgande and Alquif who awaken the heroes of olden times so that they may see the glory of the greatest of all heroes. Since Urgande is the good sorceress who replaces the *deus ex machina* of the Greek tragedies, she forms the link between the prologue and the opera proper.

Amadis tells his half-brother, Florestan, that he has chosen to follow glory rather than love because Oriane has banished him from her sight and she is, furthermore, betrothed to the King of Rome. Florestan, reunited with his love, Corisande, tells her:

Trop heureux que l'amour avec moi vous engage
Trop heureux, trop heureux de porter vos fers!
J'estime plus cent fois un si doux esclavage
Que l'empire de l'univers.[9]

She asks him why, then, must he leave her to go away in search of glory.

Fils d'un Roy dont le nom s'est partout fait connaître
Et frère d'Amadis le plus grand des héros
Pouvais-je demeurer dans un honteux repos
Aurais-je dementi le sang qui m'a fait naître?
Pour meriter de plaire aux yeux qui m'ont charmé
J'ai cherché tout l'éclat que donne la victoire.
Si j'avais moins aimé la Gloire
Vou ne m'auriez pas tant aimé.[10]

Oriane comes and complains that Amadis is unfaithful to her. If he had been willing to wait a bit, he would have been free for she must, out of duty, marry the King of Rome. (The condition of doubt is thus fulfilled because to merit their reward which the audience knows is coming, Amadis and Oriane must act out of magnanimity without thought of reward.)

The evil magicians, a brother and sister, Arcalaüs and Arcabonne, have vowed vengeance against Amadis for killing their brother, Ardan Canile. Meanwhile, Arcabonne was saved from danger by an unknown hero with whom she has fallen in love. Arcalaüs summons his demons to help capture Amadis who is just now in the dark forest. Corisande runs on stage pleading for help, and in his attempt to rescue her Amadis is taken prisoner--not by force but by the charm of beauty evoked by Arcalaüs in the shape of Oriane.

All of the heroes are now in the power of the evil magicians, and Arcabonne prepares a place for Amadis. The ghost of Ardan Canile appears and warns her that she will betray him. She denies this, but when Amadis is brought to her she recognizes him as her savior, frees all of the captives and goes off with Amadis. Arcalaüs discovers that she has not killed Amadis and threatens her that unless she does, he will unite Oriane and Amadis in front of her eyes. She becomes filled with rage at the thought and is possessed by the desire for revenge.

Entre l'amour et la haine cruelle
J'ai cru pouvoir me partager
Mais dans mon coeur l'amour est étranger
Et la haine m'est naturelle.

Arcalaüs: "Puis-je encore me fier à vous?

Fiez-vous à l'amour jaloux
Il est plus cruel que la haine.[11]

In this scene Quinault emphasizes the ideal that just as glory and the search for a good reputation must depend on magnanimity, love, also, if it is to be truly noble, must be magnanimous. He continues this theme by showing Oriane as a prisoner of Arcalaüs. She believes herself to have been abandoned by Amadis and swears that her love for him has turned to hatred. Arcalaüs makes the body of Amadis appear before her, seemingly dead, and her true feelings show. Even if he no longer cares for her, she loves him still. Just as Arcalaüs and Arcabonne are on the point of killing the lovers a flaming rock advances from the back of the stage. It changes into a ship in the form of a serpent, and Urgande and her followers arrive to rescue the good and punish the wicked. Amadis and Oriane pass through the arch of loyal lovers and enter the chamber which is forbidden to any but those whose love is entirely perfect. The enchantment is broken, the statues which formed the arch come to life, and all join in celebrating the marriage of Amadis and Oriane.

Roland

In the prologue to *Roland* a celebration in praise of Louis XIV is combined with the introduction of the story of Roland in demonstration of the errors which are committed when love is conceived for a person incapable of noble love.

Angelica of Cathay and her brother were sent by their father to stop the advance of the Christians. She had been provided with a magic ring which made her invisible when she put it into her mouth, while her brother had a magic lance which always found its mark. They were instructed to entice the Christians into a tournament by Angelica's beauty and then kill them one by one. This did not happen, but the knight Orlando (Roland), along with the other paladins, fell deeply in love with Angelica and gave her a bracelet as a token of his love. After the defeat of Angelica and her brother, she had several adventures in her wanderings and, discovering that she needed no protection since she could become invisible at will, she became very proud and disdainful of all men, including Orlando. A mere youth, unproven at arms, named Medoro received a fearful wound while attempting to bury the body of his prince. He was found by Angelica who had acquired magical skills and cured him. They stayed at a shepherd's hut, and as Medoro grew stronger, Angelica, the proud, loved and married him in that humble dwelling using the bracelet Orlando had given her as payment to the shepherds. The couple then went to Cathay. Not long afterwards, Orlando, who had gone back to fighting the Saracens with renewed fury after losing Angelica, followed a warrior into the forest close to the shepherd's hut. Lying down to rest in a shady glen he discovered inscriptions which told him that two happy lovers had passed that way. Further on, he found a lovely grotto in which Medoro had written an account of his marriage to Angelica. Orlando lost his senses for several days, and when he awakened he had gone mad and attempted to destroy everything in his path. Friendly knights found him, and he was cured by magic and brought back to the sense of his duty to his uncle, Charlemagne. Shortly after this Orlando was killed at Roncevalles.

The changes made by Quinault are confined to rearranging the chronology of the tale. He depended on previous knowledge of the story to enable the audience to know immediately the characters of Angelique and Medor. The magical element has been replaced by the motivation of ill-conceived love for though the ring of Angelique has been retained and magic is used to cure Roland, the cure is effectuated through the glorious example of heroes from previous times. The story, as Quinault told it, follows.

Angelique, queen of Cathay, is being courted by Roland but she loves Medor. She is urged to banish Medor by her servant because he is unworthy of her by birth. Angelique wishes to do so but fears that without her protection, Medor cannot survive.

Roland sends Angelique a beautiful bracelet with the message that he has given up everything for her: glory, position, honor--and his only interest in life now is winning her. She makes herself disappear, and finds Medor on the point of taking his own life. Angelique reveals her love to Medor and tells him that if he will have faith in her, she will make him King of Cathay. She returns to Roland and tries to reason with him but he, fearing he has a rival, swears to kill whomever it might be. In fear for Medor's life, Angelique assures Roland of her love. She then celebrates her marriage to Medor with the shepherds of a nearby village after which the couple flees to Cathay.

The knight, Astolphe, one of Roland's friends, comes to him and pleads with him to return to his company, reminding Roland that he should follow his glory. Roland replies that he lives only for love and even now awaits the coming of Angelique. He discovers the inscriptions, goes mad, and destroys everything he can touch. Astolphe calls the fairy, Logistille, to help bring Roland back to his senses. Logistille says she will try but it is easier to calm the elements than to calm a heart enchanted by love. Heroic Shades from the underworld are brought forth to inspire Roland through remembrance of their examples. Roland awakens filled with shame at his lack of manliness, but he is still anguished at his loss of Angelique. La Gloire, La Rénomée and La Terreur join the group of heroic Shades, and as Roland recovers his resolve to follow glory, La Gloire admonishes him never to forget the evils of an unworthy love.

Armide

Armide is the last opera written by Quinault and Lully.

In the prologue La Gloire and La Sagesse dispute which of them most loves the greatest of heroes (Louis XIV). "Maître de cent peuples divers, Plus encore maître de lui-même. Peut-on le connaître et ne l'aimer pas?"[12] They decide that he needs them both and they will go with him to see a re-enactment of the exploits of the French hero, Renaud.

Quinault has once more transformed a story so as to emphasize the ideal that glory and love must be compatible or else even the noble soul will suffer defeat. Previous knowledge of Tasso's "Jerusalem Delivered" is necessary in order to understand the situation of Armide--a warrior and unmarried, Renaud's banishment, and the identities of Ubalde, and the Danish knight--who are Renaud's companions at arms in the crusade. Other than these details, the story is understandable as Quinault wrote it, an incident in a larger drama.

The princess-warrior, Armide, has won a great victory over the crusaders and has taken many prisoners. Her father would be happy if only she were married, but she tells him that the conqueror of Renaud alone is worthy of her. In the midst of the festival a messenger arrives to tell Armide that all of her captives have been released by a single man. This can only be Renaud.

Renaud has been banished from the crusader's camp because of his defeat and performed the act of single-handed bravery in order to be reinstated. He is determined to redeem himself and will fight Armide. She traps him in an enchanted palace and is about to strike him dead with her sword when, looking at him, she falls in love with him. Since Renaud will not love her for her charms she decides to win him through enchantment. They are very happy together, but Armide cannot forget that he loves her only because of her magic. She seeks liberation from love through the demons of hatred, but in the course of their incantations she cries out to them to stop. La Haine consents but warns Armide that she will not keep Renaud because La Gloire will steal him from her, and without hatred Armide herself will be lost.

Armide returns to Renaud who assures her that glory and honor are as nothing in comparison to the sight of her eyes, but still she fears and goes to the underworld to seek counsel. During her absence, Ubalde and the Danish Knight penetrate the enchanted palace and bring Renaud to his senses. Armide returns to find that Renaud is leaving her. She tells him she will die if he does, but he cannot live for a shameful love. Though he pities her, he must leave her. Armide, alone and in despair, orders the demons to destroy the palace where she had once known happiness.

NOTES

[1]Euripides, *Alcestis*, trans. by Gilbert Murray (London: George Allen & Unwin, Ltd., 1961, pp. vii-ix.

[2]Graves, op. cit., p. 117.   The cult is also mentioned in the Bible: I Kings xv. 12 and 2 Kings xxiii. 7.

[3]Lully, *Atys* (Paris: Henri de Baussens, 1709), p. 127.

[4]At this performance, all of the King's musicians were joined by the fifes and drums of all of the regiments.   On the last beat, eighty cannons were fired simultaneously, to the terror and delight of all present.

[5]Lully, *Proserpine* (Paris: Christophe Ballard, 1714), p. 229.

[6]Ibid., p. 314.

[7]Ibid., p. 359.

[8]Grace A. Williams, "The Amadis Question," *Revue hispanique* XXI (1909), 52-58.   She lists all 258.

[9]Lully, *Oeuvres Complètes*, Les Opéras, Vol. III, pp. 50-51.

[10]Ibid., pp. 51-52.

[11]Ibid., pp. 171-72.

[12]Lully, *Armide* (Paris: Christophe Ballard, 1713), p. 3.

APPENDIX IV

STRUCTURE OF SCENES

Cadmus et Hermione

Prologue.
  Scenes:
    1.   Scene-complex.
    2.   "
    3.   "
    4.   "
    5.   "

Act I.
  Scenes:
    1.   Recitative-dialogue.
    2.   "
    3.   "
    4.   Scene-complex.
    5.   Recitative-dialogue.
    6.   "

Act II.
  Scenes:
    1.   Recitative-dialogue.
    2.   "
    3.   "
    4.   "
    5.   Air.
    6.   Scene-complex.

Act III.
  Scenes:
    1.   Recitative-dialogue.
    2.   "
    3.   "
    4.   Recitative-monologue.
    5.   Scene-complex.
    6.   "
    7.   "

Act. IV.
    Scenes:
        1.   Recitative-dialogue.
        2.   Scene-complex.
        3.   "
        4.   "
        5.   "
        6.   "
        7.   "

Act V.
    Scenes:
        1.   Recitative-monologue.
        2.   Recitative-dialogue.
        3.   Scene-complex.

Alceste

Prologue.
    Scene-complex.
Act I.
    Scenes:
        1.   Recitative-dialogue (the chorus is present and sings, but the scene is basically dialogue).
        2.   Trio.
        3.   Recitative-dialogue.
        4.   "
        5   "
        6.   Scene-complex.
        7.   "
        8.   "

Act II.
    Scenes:
        1.   Recitative-dialogue.
        2.   " (followed by the beginning of the war).
        3.   Scene-complex.
        4.   "
        5.   Recitative, air.
        6.   Recitative-dialogue.

7.   Trio.
8.   Recitative-dialogue.
9.   Recitative-monologue (but with spectacle).

Act. III
    Scenes:
      1.   Recitative-dialogue.
      2.   Scene-complex.
      3.   "
      4.   "
      5.   "
      6.   Recitative-monologue.
      7.   Recitative-dialogue.
      8.   Recitative-monologue (with spectacle).

Act IV.
    Scenes:
      1.   Scene-complex.
      2.   Recitative-dialogue.
      3.   Scene-complex.
      4.   "
      5.   "

Act V.
    Scenes:
      1.   Scene-complex.
      2.   Recitative, air, duet.
      3.   Scene-complex.
      4.   "
      5.   "
      6.   "

Thésée

Prologue.
    Scene-complex.
Act I.
    Scenes:
      1.   Scene-complex.
      2.   "
      3.   Recitative-dialogue.
      4.   Scene-complex.

      5.   "

      6.   "

      7.   "

      8.   "

Act. II.

    Scenes:

        1.   Recitative-dialogue.

        2.   "

        3.   "

        4.   "

        5.   Air.

        6.   Scene-complex.

        7.   Recitative-dialogue.

        8.   "

        9.   "

Act III.

    Scenes:

        1.   Recitative-dialogue.

        2.   "

        3.   "

        4.   Recitative-dialogue.

        5.   "

        6.   Scene-complex.

        7.   "

        8.   "

Act IV.

    Scenes:

        1.   Recitative-dialogue.

        2.   "

        3.   "

        4.   "

        5.   "

        6.   "

        7.   Scene-complex.

Act V.

    Scenes:

        1.   Recitative-monologue.

        2.   Recitative-dialogue.

        3.   "

    4.   Scene-complex.
    5.   "
    6.   "
    7.   "
    8.   "

Atys

Prologue.
    Scene-complex.

Act I.
    Scenes:
        1.   Recitative-monologue.
        2.   Recitative-dialogue.
        3.   "
        4.   "
        5.   "
        6.   "
        7.   Scene-complex.

Act II.
    Scenes:
        1.   Recitative-dialogue.
        2.   "
        3.   "
        4.   Scene-complex.

Act III.
    Scenes:
        1.   Recitative-monologue.
        2.   Recitative-dialogue.
        3.   Recitative-monologue.
        4.   Scene-complex.
        5.   Recitative-dialogue.
        6.   Recitative-dialogue.
        7.   "
        8.   Recitative-monologue.

Act IV.
    Scenes:
        1.   Recitative-dialogue.
        2.   "
        3.   "
        4.   "
        5.   Scene-complex.
        6.   "

Act V.
    Scenes:
        1.   Recitative-dialogue.
        2.   "
        3.   Scene-complex.
        4.   "
        5.   "
        6.   "
        7.   "

Isis

Prologue.
    Scenes:
        1.   Scene-complex.
        2.   "
        3.   "

Act I.
    Scenes:
        1.   Recitative-monologue.
        2.   Recitative-dialogue.
        3.   "
        4.   "
        5.   Scene-complex.
        6.   "

Act II.
    Scenes:
        1.   Recitative-monologue.
        2.   Recitative-dialogue.
        3.   "

      4.   Recitative-dialogue.
      5.   Recitative, aria.
      6.   Scene-complex.
      7.   "
      8.   "

Act III.
Scenes:
      1.   Recitative-dialogue.
      2.   "
      3.   Scene-complex.
      4.   "
      5.   "
      6.   "
      7.   "
      8.   "

Act IV.
Scenes:
      1.   Scene-complex.
      2.   "
      3.   "
      4.   "
      5.   "
      6.   "

Act V.
Scenes:
      1.   Recitative-monologue.
      2.   Recitative-dialogue.
      3.   Scene-complex.

Psyché

Prologue.
Scenes:
      1.   Scene-complex.
      2.   "
      3.   "

Act I.
      Scenes:
          1.   Recitative-dialogue.
          2.   Scene-complex.
          3.   Recitative-dialogue.
          4.   "

Act II.
      Scenes:
          1.   Recitative-monologue.
          2.   Recitative-dialogue.
          3.   "
          4.   Recitative-dialogue.
          5.   Scene-complex.
          6.   "
          7.   "

Act III.
      Scenes:
          1.   Recitative-monologue.
          2.   Recitative-dialogue.
          3.   "
          4.   Recitative-monologue.
          5.   Recitative-dialogue.
          6.   Recitative-monologue.
          7.   Recitative-dialogue.

Act IV.
      Scenes:
          1.   Recitative-monologue.
          2.   Scene-complex.
          3.   "

Act V.
      Scenes:
          1.   Recitative-monologue.
          2.   Recitative-dialogue.
          3.   "
          4.   Scene-complex.

Bellérophon

Prologue.
>   Scene-complex.

Act I.
>   Scenes:
>>   1.   Recitative-dialogue.
>>   2.   "
>>   3.   "
>>   4.   "
>>   5.   Scene-complex.

Act II.
>   Scenes:
>>   1.   Recitative-dialogue.
>>   2.   "
>>   3.   "
>>   4.   "
>>   5.   "
>>   6.   Recitative-monologue.
>>   7.   Scene-complex.

Act III.
>   Scenes:
>>   1.   Recitative-dialogue.
>>   2.   "
>>   3.   "
>>   4.   "
>>   5.   Scene-complex.
>>   6.   Recitative-dialogue.

Act IV.
>   Scenes:
>>   1.   Recitative-monologue.
>>   2.   Recitative-dialogue.
>>   3.   "
>>   4.   "
>>   5.   "
>>   6.   Recitative-monologue.
>>   7.   Scene-complex.

Act V.
    Scenes:
        1.   Scene-complex.
        2.   "
        3.   "

Proserpine

Prologue.
    Scenes:
        1.   Scene-complex.
        2.   "

Act I.
    Scenes:
        1.   Recitative-dialogue.
        2.   "
        3.   "
        4.   Air and recitative-dialogue.
        5.   Recitative-dialogue.
        6.   Scene-complex.
        7.   "

Act II.
    Scenes:
        1.   Recitative-dialogue.
        2.   "
        3.   Recitative-monologue.
        4.   Recitative-dialogue.
        5.   "
        6.   "
        7.   "
        8.   Scene-complex.
        9.   "

Act III.
    Scenes:
        1.   Scene-complex.
        2.   Recitative-dialogue.
        3.   Scene-complex.

4. Scene-complex.
5.   "
6.   "
7.   "
8.   "

Act IV.
 Scenes:
  1. Scene-complex.
  2.   "
  3.   "
  4. Recitative-dialogue.
  5. Scene-complex.

Act V.
 Scenes:
  1. Scene-complex.
  2. Recitative-monologue.
  3. Scene-complex.
  4.   "
  5.   "
  6.   "

Persée

Prologue.
 Scene-complex.

Act I.
 Scenes:
  1. Recitative-dialogue.
  2.   "
  3. Recitative-monologue.
  4. Scene-complex. (Begins with long recitative-dialogue.)
  5.   "

Act II.
 Scenes:
  1. Recitative-dialogue.
  2. Scene-complex.
  3.   "
  4. Recitative-monologue.
  5. Recitative-dialogue.
  6.   "
  7. Recitative-monologue.

8. Scene-complex.
9.   "

Act III.
    Scenes:
      1. Recitative-dialogue.
      2. Scene-complex.
      3.   "
      4.   "
      5.   "

Act IV.
    Scenes:
      1. Scene-complex.
      2. Recitative-dialogue.
      3. Scene-complex.
      4.   "
      5.   "
      6.   "

Act V.
    Scenes:
      1. Recitative-monologue.
      2. Recitative-dialogue.
      3. Scene-complex.
      4   "
      5.   "
      6. Scene-complex.
      7.   "
      8.   "

Phaéton

Prologue.
    Scene-complex.

Act I.
    Scenes:
      1. Recitative-monologue.
      2. Recitative-dialogue.
      3. Recitative-dialogue.
      4.   "
      5. Scene-complex.
      6.   "
      7.   "
      8.   "

Act II.
    Scenes:
        1.   Recitative dialogue.
        2.   Aria.
        3.   Recitative-dialogue.
        4.   "
        5.   Scene-complex.

Act III.
    Scenes:
        1.   Recitative-dialogue.
        2.   Recitative-monologue.
        3.   Recitative-dialogue.
        4.   Scene-complex.
        5.   "
        6.   Recitative-dialogue.

Act IV.
    Scene:
        1.   Scene-complex.
        2.   "

Act V.
    Scenes:
        1.   Recitative-dialogue.
        2.   "
        3.   "
        4.   Scene-complex.
        5.   "
        6.   "

Amadis

Prologue.
    Scene-complex.

Act I.
    Scenes:
        1.   Recitative-dialogue.
        2.   "
        3.   "
        4.   Scene-complex.

Act II.
    Scenes:
        1.   Air.
        2.   Recitative-dialogue.

        3.   Recitative-monologue.
        4.   Air.
        5.   Recitative-dialogue.
        6.   Scene-complex.
        7.   "

Act III.
        Scenes:
        1.   Scene-complex.
        2.   "
        3.   "
        4.   "

Act IV.
        Scenes:
        1.   Recitative-dialogue.
        2.   Recitative-monologue.
        3.   Recitative-dialogue.
        4.   Recitative-monologue.
        5.   Recitative-dialogue.
        6.   Scene-complex.

Act V.
        Scenes:
        1.   Recitative-dialogue.
        2.   "
        3.   Recitative-dialogue.
        4.   Scene-complex.
        5.   "

Roland

Prologue.
        Scene-complex.

Act I.
        Scenes:
        1.   Recitative-monologue.
        2.   Recitative-dialogue.
        3.   Recitative-monologue.
        4.   Recitative-dialogue.
        5.   "
        6.   Scene-complex.

Act II.
        Scenes:
        1.   Scene-complex.

2.   "
3.   Recitative-dialogue.
4.   "
5.   Scene-complex.

Act III.
    Scenes:
    1.   Recitative-dialogue.
    2.   "
    3.   "
    4.   Scene-complex.
    5.   "

Act IV.
    Scenes:
    1.   Recitative-dialogue.
    2.   Recitative-monologue.
    3.   Scene-complex.
    4.   "
    5.   "
    6.   Recitative-monologue.

Act V.
    Scenes:
    1.   Scene-complex.
    2.   "
    3.   "
    4.   "

Armide

Prologue.
    Scene-complex.

Act I.
    Scenes:
    1.   Recitative-dialogue.
    2.   "
    3.   Scene-complex.
    4.   "

Act II.
    Scenes:
    1.   Recitative-dialogue.
    2.   "
    3.   Recitative-monologue.
    4.   Scene-complex.

5. Recitative-monologue.

Act III.
Scenes:
1. Recitative-monologue.
2. Recitative-dialogue.
3. Aria.
4. Scene-complex.

Act IV.
Scenes:
1. Scene-complex.
2. "
3. "
4. "

Act V.
Scenes:
1. Recitative-dialogue.
2. Scene-complex.
3. Recitative-dialogue.
4. Scene-complex.
5. "

APPENDIX V

MUSICAL EXCERPTS

In the four scenes from *Psyché, Alceste, Roland and Persée* modern clef signs have been substituted for the originals. Meter signs, figured bass, ornaments and verbal instructions are preserved as given in the original printings.

Each scene is preceded by a copy of the text with numbers indicating Lully's syllabification.

PSYCHE ACT III, ii

Psché:	Que fais-tu? montre-toy, cher objet de ma flâme,	13
	Vien consoler mon âme.	7
	La beauté de ces lieux est un enchantement,	12
	Tout m'y paroit charmant;	6
	Mais je n'y vois point ce que j'aime	9
	(Repeat the last three lines.)	
	Ah qu'une absence d'un moment,	8
	Quand la tendresse est extrême,	9
	Est un rigoureux tourment!	7
	(Repeat three lines, different music.)	
	(She sees Venus.)	
	Par quel art, dans ce lieu, vous rendez-vous visible?	13
	On m'y parle souvent, sans qu'on s'y laisse vior.	12
Venus:	Le Dieu que vos beautez ont rendu si sensible,	12
	Pour vous entretenir m'a laissé ce pouvoir.	12
	C'est à moy, Psché, qu'il ordonne	9
	De garder ce Palais où tout suit vôtre loy.	12
Psché:	Nymphe, le croiriez vous, que luy-même empoisonne	13
	Tous les honneurs que j'en reçoy?	8
	Il refuse toujours de se montrer à moy,	12
	Dans tout l'éclat qui l'environne;	9
	Et ce refus blesse ma foy.	8
	Je l'aime et je voudrois pouvoir tout sur son âme,	13
	Je voudrois avoir lieu du moins de m'en flatter,	12
	Quand je forme des voeux qu'il ose rebuter,	12
	Je suis réduite à douter de ma flâme;	11
	Et rien n'est plus cruel pour moy que d'en douter.	12
Venus:	Mais chaque instant vous marque sa tendresse.	11
	Ah! Malgré les soupirs qu'un Amant nous adresse;	13
	Malgré tous les soins qu'il nous rend,	8
	Il ne faut, pour troubler le bonheur le plus grand,	12
	Qu'un peu trop de delicatesse.	9
	Vous n'êtes pas les plus heureux,	8
	Vous dont l'amour est si pur et si tendre,	11
	Si tout votre repos est reduit à dependre	13

	Du moindre scrupule amoureux;	8
	Vous dont l'amour est si pur et si tendre,	11
	Vous n'êtes pas les plus heureux!	8
	Que ne m'est-il pas permis de vous tirer de peine!	13
Pysché:	Ah! Ne me tenez point plus longtemps incertaine	13
	Satisfaites mes yeux,	6
	Vous avez ce pouvoir.	6
Venus:	Vous me découvrirez.	6
Pysché:	Ne craignez rien.	11
Venus:	Je n'ose.	3
Pysché:	Quoy, rien en ma faveur ne peut vous émouvior?	12
Venus:	Et bien, je vais pour vous, oublier mon devoir.	12
	Entrez, C'est dans ce lieu que vôtre Amant repose,	13
	Goutez, Goutez, le plaisir de le voir.	10
	Cette lampe que je vous laisse,	9
	Peut servir à vous eclairer.	8
Pysché:	Que ne vous dois-je point	6
Venus:	Il faut me retirer:	
	Ma présence nuiroit au désir qui vous presse.	13

Psyché sans voir Venus
Que fais- tu? mon-tre

toi, cher ob- jet de ma flâ-me, Viens con-so ler mon a ——

Vous dont l'a—mour est si pur et—si ten—dre; Si tout vô—tre re—pos est re—duit à dé—pen—dre Du moin—dre scru—pu—le a—mou—reux; Vous dont l'a—mour est si pur et—si ten—dre, Vous n'ê—tes pas les plus heu—reux. Que ne m'est-il per—

ALCESTE ACT I, iv

Céphise:	Dans ce beau jour, quelle humeur sombre	9
	Fais-tu voir à contre Temps?	7
Straton:	C'est que je ne suis pas du nombre	9
	Des amants qui sont contents.	7
Céphise:	Un ton grondeur et sévère	8
	N'est pas un grand agrément;	7
	Le chagrin n'avance guère	8
	Les affaires d'un amant,	7
	Le chagrin n'avance guère	8
	Les affaires d'un amant,	7
	Le chagrin etc.	8
Straton:	Lychas vient de me faire entendre	9
	Que je n'ai plus ton coeur,	6
	Qu'il doit seul y prétendre,	7
	Et que tu ne vois plus mon amour qu'à regret.	12
Céphise:	Lychas est peu discret. . .	6
Straton:	Ah! Je m'en doutois bien qu'il voulois me	
	surprendre.	13
Céphise:	Lychas est peu discret	6
	D'avoir dit mon secret.	6
Straton:	Comment! il est donc vrai! tu n'en fais	
	point d'excuse?	13
	Tu me trahis ainsi, sans en être confuse?	13
Céphise:	Tu te plains sans raison;	6
	Est-ce une trahison	6
	Quand on te désabuse?	7
Straton:	Que je suis étonné de voir ton changement.	12
Céphise:	Si je change d'amant	6
	Qu'y trouves-tu d'étrange!	7
	(Repeat first two lines.)	
	Est-ce un sujet d'étonnement	8

De voir une fille qui change.   9
De voir une fille qui change.   9
(Repeat the last three lines.)

Straton: Après deux ans passés, dans un si doux lien,*   12
           Devois-tu jamais prendre une chaine
               nouvelle?   13

Céphise: Ne contes-tu pour rien   6
           D'etre deux ans fidèle?   7

Straton: Par un espoir doux et trompeur   8
           Pourquoi m'engageois-tu dans un amour,   11
           Dans un amour si tendre!   7
           Faloit-il me donner ton coeur   8
           Puisque tu voulois le reprendre?   9
           (Repeat the last two lines.)

Céphise: Quand je t'offrois mon coeur, c'était de
               bonne foi,   12
           Que n'empêches-tu qu'on te l'ôte?   9
           Est-ce ma faute,   5
           Est-ce ma faute   5
           Si Lychas me plaît plus que toi?   8
           (Repeat the last three lines.)

Straton: Ingrate, est-ce le prix de ma persévèrance?   14

Céphise: Essaye un peu de l'inconstance   9
       .   Essaye un peu de l'inconstance;   9
           C'est toi qui le premier m'appris à m'engager,   12
           Pour récompense,   5
           Pour récompense,   5
           Je te veux apprendre à changer.   8
           (Repeat the last three lines.)

                      /changer\
Together: Il faut   toujours   6
                      \aimer /

(Repeat five times.)

_____
*Two notes for lien.

Les plus douces amours

Sont les amours〈nouvelles.   7
                 fidèles.
(Repeat three times.)

Then, repeat the first line five times once again.

ROLAND ACT IV, ii

Roland:	Ah! j'attendray longtemps, la nuit est loin encore,	13
	Quoy, le soleil veut-il luire toujours?	10
	Jaloux de mon bonheur, il prolonge son cours.	12
	Pour retarder la Beauté que j'adore.	11
	O Nuit! favorisez mes désirs amourex.	12
	Pressez l'Astre du jour de descendre dans l'Onde;	13
	Dépliez dans les airs vos voiles ténébreux,	12
	Je ne troubleray plus par mes cris doulereux	12
	Vostre tranquilité profonde.	9
	Le charmant Objet de mes voeux	8
	N'attent que vous pour rendre heureux	8
	Le plus fidelle Amant de Monde.	9
	O Nuit! favorisez mes désirs amoureux.	12
	Que ces gazons sont verds!	6
	Que cette grotte est belle!	7
	Ce que je lis m'apprend que l'amour a	
	conduit	12
	Dans ce boccage loin du bruit,	8
	Deux Amants qui bruloient d'une ardeur	
	mutuelle.	13
	J'espère qu'avec moy l'Amour bientost icy	12
	Conduira la Beauté que j'aime.	9
	Enchantez d'un bonheur extrême	9
	Sur ces Grottes bientost nous escrirons	
	aussi.	12
	Beaus lieux, doux azile	6
	De nos heureuses amours,	7
	Puissiez vous estre toujours	7
	Charmant et tranquille.	6
	Voyons tout.	3
	Qu'est-ce que je voy?	5
	Ces mots semblent tracez de la main	
	d'Angelique.	13
	Ciel! c'est pour un autre que moi	9
	Que Son Amour s'explique.	7
	Angelique engage son coeur,	8
	Medor en est vainquer.	6
	Elle m'auroit flatté d'une vain esperance?	13
	L'Ingrate! N'est-ce point un soupçon qui	
	l'offence?	13
	Medor est en vainquer!	6

Non, je n'ay point encore   6
Entendu parler de Medor.   8
Mon amour auroit lieu de prendre des
    allarmes   13
Si je trouvois icy le nom   8
De l'intrepide fils d'Aimon,   8
Ou quelqu'autre Guerrier célèbre pour les
    armes.   13
Angelique n'a pas osé   8
Avouer de son coeur le véritable Maistre.   13
Et je puis aisément connaistre   9
Qu'elle parle de moy sous un nom supposé.   12
C'est pour moy seul qu'elle soupire,   9
Elle me l'a trop dit, et j'en suis trop
    certain.   12
Lisons ces autres, ils sont d 'un autre main. . .   12
Qu'ai-je leu? Ciel! Il faut relire. . .   9
Que Medor est heureux!   6
Angelique a comblé ses voeux.   8
Ce Medor quelqu'il soit se donne ici la
    gloire   13
D'estre l'heureux Vainqueur d'un objet si
    charmant   12
Angelique a comblé les voeux d'un autre
    amant?   12
Elle a pu me trahir?   6
Non, je ne le puis croire,   7
Non, non, quelqu'Envieux a voulu par ces
    mots   12
Noircir l'Objet que j'aime et troubler mon
    repos.   12
J'entens un bruit de Musique champestre,   11
Il faut chercher Angelique en ces lieux.   10
Au premier regard de ses yeus   8
Mes noirs soupçons vont disparaistre.   9

Elle s'arrestera peut-estre   9

A voir danser au son des Chalumeaux   10
Les Bergers des prochains Hameaux   8

(Repeat the last three lines.)

Mon— de. O nuit! fa-vo-ri-sez mes dé-sirs a-mou-

reux.

mants qui bru- loient d'une ar - deur mu-tu- el- le. J'és-

pé- requ'a-vec moy l'A-mour bien-tost i- cy con- dui-

Je n'ai point en-co— re En-ten-du par—ler de Me—dor. Mon a— mour au-roit lieu de pren-dre des al—

Au pre—mier re—gard de ses yeux Mes noirs soup-çons vont dis — pa-

raîs- tre.   El- le s'ar-res-te-ra   peut— es — tre A

voir dan-ser au son des Cha-lu- meaux Les Ber-

ger des pro-chains Ha- meaux.

PERSEE ACT IV, iii

Deux Ethiopiens et Idas: O ciel inexorable!		7
	O malheur déplorable!	7
Tous:	O ciel inexorable!	7
	O malheur déplorable!	7
Seul:	O ciel inexorable!	7
Tous:	O malheur déplorable!	7
Merope et Phinée: Qui pouroit traverser ces trop		
	heureux Amants?	12
	D'où viennent vos gemissements?	8
Idas:	L'implacable Junon cause nostre infortune;	13
	Elle arme contre nous l'Empire de Neptune;	12
	Un Monstre en doit sortir,	6
	Qui viendra dévorer l'innocente Andromède,	13
	Et Thétis et ses Soeurs viennent de	
	déclarer,	12
	Qu 'il n'est plus permis d'éspérer,	8
	De voir finir nos maux sans ce cruel remède.	13
	Les Tritons ont saisi la Princesse à nos	
	yeux,	12
	Et le pouvior des Dieux	6
	Nous a rendu tous immobiles.	9
	C'est sur ces bords qu'au Monstre on la	
	doit exposer,	12
	Pour son secours Persée en vain veut tout	
	oser,	12
	Ses efforts seront inutiles.	9
	Il faut céder aux Dieux	7
	Il faut céder au sort,	6
	Dont Andromède est poursuivie;	9
	Croyoit-on voir finir une si belle vie,	13
	Par une si terrible mort?	8
Deux Ethiopiens et Idas: O sort inexorable!		7

Tous: O malheur déplorable!   7

Deux Ethiopiens et Idas: Princesse infortunée helas!   9
            Vous meritiez un sort favorable,   11
            Vous ne meritiez pas   6
            Un si cruel trépas.   6
            O sort inexorable!   7
            O malheur déplorable!   7

Tous: O sort inexorable!   7
            O malheur déplorable!   7

            (The same two lines are then divided
               between the soloists and the choeur.)

Phinée: Les Dieux ont soin de nous venger;   8
            Le plaisir que je sens avec peine se cache?   13
Merope: Verrez-vous sans douleur Andromède en danger?   12

Phinée: Est-ce à moi que l'Amour l'arrache?   9
            C'est à Persee à s'affliger.   8
            L'Amour meurt dans mon coeur,   6
            La rage luy succède   7
            (Repeat the last two lines.)
            J'ayme mieux voir un Monstre affreux   8
            Dévorer l'ingrate Andromède,   9
            Que la voir dans les bras de mon Rival
               heureux.   12
            (Repeat the last three lines.)

SELECTED BIBLIOGRAPHY

Musical Sources

The following scores were used.

Lully, Jean-Baptiste de. *Alceste.* Ser. III, Vol. II of *Oeuvres Complètes.* Edited by Henry Prunières. Paris: Editions de la Revue musicale, 1932.

_____. *Amadis.* Ser. III, Vol. III of *Oeuvres Complètes.* Edited by Henry Prunières. Paris: Editions Lully, 1939.

_____. *Armide.* 2nd ed. Paris: Jean-Christophe Ballard, 1713.

_____. *Atys.* 2nd ed. Paris: Henri de Baussens, 1709.

_____. *Bellérophon.* 2nd ed. Paris: Jean-Christophe Ballard, 1714.

_____. *Cadmus et Hermione.* Ser. III, Vol. I of *Oeuvres Complètes.* Edited by Henry Prunières. Paris: Editions de la Revue musicale, 1930.

_____. *Isis.* Paris: Jean-Christophe Ballard, 1719.

_____. *Persée.* Paris: Jean-Christophe Ballard, 1682.

_____. *Phaéton.* Paris: Jean-Christophe Ballard, 1683.

_____. *Proserpine.* 2nd ed. Paris: Jean-Christophe Ballard, 1714.

_____. *Psyché.* Paris: Jean-Christophe Ballard, 1720.

_____. *Roland.* Paris: Jean-Christophe Ballard, 1685.

_____. *Thésée.* Paris: Jean-Christophe Ballard, 1688.

Also consulted:

Les Chefs d'oeuvres classiques de l'opéra français. Vols. 13-26. Edited by Théodore de Lajarte. Leipzig: Breitkopf & Hartel, 1880. (This edition contains all thirteen of the *Tragédies lyriques* and incorporates the cuts and changes made during the century they were performed rather than going back to the first printings.)

Lully and the *Tragédie Lyrique*

Achenwall, Max. *Studien über die komische Oper in Frankreich im 18. Jahrhundert und ihre Beziehungen zu Molière.* Eilenburg: Offenhauer, 1912.

Adam, Adolphe. *Souvenirs d'un musicien.* Paris: Calmann-Levy, 1884.

Ademollo, Alessandro. *I primi fasti della musica italiana a Parigi (1645-1662).* Milano: Ricordi, 1884.

Albert, Maurice. *Les Théâtres de la foire (1600-1789)*. Paris: Hachette, 1900.

Aldrich, Putnam C.   "The Principal Agréments of the Seventeenth and Eighteenth Centuries; a Study in Musical Ornamentation." Unpublished Ph.D. dissertation, Harvard University, 1942.

Altmann, Charlotte.   "Der französische Einfluss auf die Textbücher der klassischen Wiener Operette." Unpublished Ph.D. dissertation, University of Vienna, 1935.

L'Ancienne France . . . le théâtre, mystères, tragédie, comédie et la musique. Instruments-ballet-opéra jusqu'en 1789. Paris: Firmin-Didot, 1887.

Anthony, James R. *French Baroque Music.* New York: W. W. Norton, 1974.

Arger, Jane. *Les Agréments et le rhythme; leur représentation graphique dans la musique vocale française du XVIIe siècle.* Paris: Rouart, Lerolle, 1917.

_____. "Le Role expressif des 'agréments' dans l'école vocale française de 1680 a 1760." *Revue de musicologie,* I (1917-1919), 215-26.

Arnheim, Amalie. "Ein Beitrag zur Geschichte des einstimmigen weltlichen Kunstliedes in Frankreich im 17. Jahrhundert." *Sammelbände der internationalen Musikgesellschaft,* X (1908-1909), 399-421.

Arnold, Frank T. *The Art of Accompaniment from a Thorough-Bass as Practiced in the XVIIth and XVIIIth Centuries.* London: Oxford University Press, 1931.

Aubin, Leon. *Le Drame lyrique; histoire de la musique dramatique en France.* Tours: édition de l'Echo littéraire et artistique, 1908.

Bekker, Paul. *The Orchestra.* New York: W. W. Norton & Company, 1963.

Bellaigue, Camille. *Paroles et musique.* Paris: Perrin, 1925.

Benham, Evelyn. "A Musical Monopolist (J. B. Lully)." *Music and Letters,* IX (1928) 249-54.

Benoit, M. *Versailles et les musiciens du Roi. 1661-1733: étude institutionelle et sociale.* Paris: Picard, 1971.

Benvenga, Nancy. "Drottningholm Discovery." *Opera* 26 (Autumn 1975):114-15.

Bérard, Jean Antoine. *L'Art du chant.* Paris: Dessait & Saillant, 1755.

Bertolotti, Antonio. *Artisti francesi in Roma nei secolo XV, XVI e XVII.* Mantua: Mondovi, 1894.

Bethléem, Abbé L., and others. *Les Opéras, les opéras-comiques et les opérettes.* Paris: Editions de la Revue des lectures, 1926.

Blasis, Carlo. *Della musica dramatica italiana in Francia, e della musica francese dal secolo XVII sino al principio del secolo XIX.* Milano: Gugliemi e Redaelli, 1841.

Blaze (François Henri Joseph), called Castil-Blaze. *L'Académie impériale de musique. . .de 1645 a 1855.* Paris: Castil-Blaze,   1855.

_____. *De l'opéra en France.* Paris: Janet et Cotelle, 1820.

Bobillier, Marie. *Les Concerts en France sous l'ancien régime.* Paris: Fischbacher, 1900.

Boislisle, Arthur Michel de.   "Les Débuts de l'opéra francais à Paris." *Mémoires de la Société de l'histoire de Paris,* II (1876) 172 ff.

Boll, André.   "L'Art lyrique: évolution du récitatif." *Revue musicale,* N. 217 (1952) 19-32.

_____.   "Les Musiciens de Molière." *Courier musical de France* 42 (1973):46-47.

Borland, John E.   "French Opéra before 1750." *Proceedings of the Musical Association,* XXXIII (1907) 133-57.

Borowitz, Albert I.   "Lully and the Death of Cambert." *Music Review* 35 (1974):231-39.

Borrel, Eugène. *L'Interprétation de la musique française (de Lully) à la révolution.* Paris: F. Alcan, 1924.

_____.   "L'Interprétation de l'ancien récitatif français," *Revue de musicologie,* XII (1931) 13-21.

_____.   "L'Interprétation de Lully d'après Rameau," *Revue de Musicologie,* XII (1929), 17-25.

_____.   "Les Notes inégales dans l'ancienne musique française." *Revue de Musicologie,* XII (1931) 278-89.

_____. *Lully.* Paris: Euterpe, 1947.

Böttger, Friedrich. *Die "Comédie-Ballet" von Molière-Lully.* Berlin: Funk, 1931.

Bragard, Roger, and de Hen, J. Ferdinand. *Musical Instruments in Art and History.* Translated by Bill Hopkins.   New York: The Viking Press, 1967.

Bricqueville, Eugène de. *Le Livret d'opéra français de Lully à Gluck.* Bruxelles: 1888.

Campardon, Emil. *L'Académie royale de musique au XVIIIe siècle.* Paris: Berger-Levrault, 1884.

_____. *Les Spectacles des foires. . .depuis 1595 jusqu'à 1791.* Paris: Berger-Levrault, 1877.

Carse, Adam. *The History of Orchestration.* New York: Dover, 1964.

Chailley, Jacques.   "La Declamation théâtrale aux XVIIe et XVIIIe siècles d'après les récitatifs." *Saggi e ricerche in memoria di Ettore Li Gotti* (Centro di Studi filologici e linguistici siciliani, *Bolletino,* 6.   Palermo, 1962), 355-57.

_____. "Notes sur la famille de Lully." *Revue de musicologie*, XXXIVV (1952), 103-104.

Champigneulle, Bernard. "L'Influence de Lully hors de France." *Revue musicale*, XXII (February-March, 1946), 26-35.

Chisholm, Duncan. "Thésée." *Musical Times* 117 (June 1976):505.

Christout, Marie-Françoise. *Le Ballet de cour de Louis XIV 1643-1672*. Paris: A. et J. Picard et Cie., 1967.

Chouquet, Gustave. *Histoire de la musique dramatique en France*. Paris: Firmin Didot, 1873.

Chumbley, Joyce Arlene. "The World of Molière's comédie-ballets." Ph.D. dissertation, University of Hawaii, 1972.

Combarieu, Jules. "Histoire du théâtre lyrique." *Revue d'histoire et de critique musicale*, VII (1907), 581-97; VIII (1908), 1-594 *passim;* IX (1909) *passim;* X (1910) *passim.*

Cordey, Jean. "Lully d'après l'inventaire de ses biens." *Revue de musicologie*, XXXVII (July, 1935).

Courville, Xavier de. "Quinault poète d'opéra." *Revue musicale*, VI (January, 1925), 74-88.

Crichton, Ronald. "Jean-Baptiste de Lully." *Ballet*, II (1939), 30-32.

Denizard, Marie. "La Famille française de Lully." *Mercure musical*, VIII, No. 5 (1912), 1-14.

Demuth, Norman. *French Opera*. Sussex: The Artemis Press, Ltd., 1963.

Deshayes, A. J. J. *Idées générales sur l'Académie royale de musique, et plus spécialement sur la danse*. Paris: Mongie, 1822.

Dumesnil, René. *Histoire illustrée du théâtre lyrique*. Paris: Plan, 1953.

Ecorcheville, Jules. "Corneille et la musique." *Courrier musical*, IX (1906), 405-12, 438-49.

_____. *De Lulli à Rameau, 1690-1730; l'esthétique musicale*. Paris: Fortin, 1906.

_____. "Lully gentilhomme et sa descendance." *Mercure musical*, VII, No. 5 (1911), 1-19; No. 6, 1-27; No. 7, 36-52.

Ellison, Mary B. *"The Comparaison de la musique Italienne et de la musique Françoise* of Lecerf de la Viéville: an annotated translation of the first four dialogues." Ph.D. dissertation, University of Miami, 1973.

Eppelsheim, Jürgen. *Das Orchester in den Werken Jean-Baptiste Lully*. Tutzing: H. Schneider, 1961.

Fabian, I. "Ein Meisterwerk der fruehen franzozischen Oper-Lullys *'Alceste'* unter Jean-Claude Malgloire." Opernwelt 17 (May 1976):15.

Filippi, Joseph de. *Parallèle des principaux théâtres modernes de l'Europe et des machines théâtrales françaises, allemandes et anglaises.* Paris: Levy, 1870.

Font, Auguste. *Favart, l'opéra-comique et la comédie-vaudeville aux XVIIe et XVIIIe siècles.* Paris: Fischbacher, 1894.

Forbes, Elizabeth. "*Alceste* London Opera Center." *Opera* 27 (February 1976):182-83.

Gerold, Théodore. *L'Art du chant en France au XVIIe siècle.* Strasbourg: G. Fischbach, 1921.

Girdlestone, Cuthbert. *La Tragédie lyrique en musique, 1673-1750, considéré comme un genre littéraire.* Genève: Droz, 1972.

Goddard, Joseph. *The Rise and Development of Opera; embracing a comparative view of the art in Italy, Germany, France, and England* New York: Scribner's, 1912.

Goldschmidt, Hugo. "Die Instrumentalbegleitung der italienischen Musikdramen in der ersten Hälfte des XVII. Jahrhunderts." *Monatshefte für Musikgeschichte,* XXVII (1895), 52-62.

_____. *Die Lehre von der vokalen Ornamentik.* Erster Band: Das 17. und 18. Jahrhundert bis in die Zeit Glucks. Charlottenburg: Lehsten, 1907.

_____. "Zur Geschichte der Arien-und Symphonie-Formen." *Monatshefte für Musikgeschichte,* XXXIII (1901), 61-70.

Grégoir, Edouard. *Des Gloires de l'opéra et la musique à Paris.* Bruxelles: Schott, 1878.

Gros, Etienne. *Philippe Quinault.* Paris: Librairie Ancienne Honoré Champion. Aix-en-Provence: Editions du "Feu," 1926.

Grout, Donald J. "German Baroque Opera." *The Musical Quarterly* XXXII (1946), 574-87.

_____. "The Machine Operas." *Bulletin of the Fogg Museum of Art,* Harvard University, IX, No. 5 (November, 1941), 100-103.

_____. "The Music of the Italian Theater at Paris, 1692-1697," *Papers of the American Musicological Society* (1946), 158-70.

_____. "Origins of the Opéra-comique." Unpublished Ph.D. dissertation, Harvard University, 1939.

_____. "Seventeenth Century Parodies of French Opera." *The Musical Quarterly,* XXVII (1941), 211-19, 514-26.

_____. "Some Forerunners of the Lully Opera." *Music and Letters,* XXII (1941), 1-25.

_____. *A Short History of Opera.* New York: Columbia University Press, 1947. Second edition, 1968.

Hargrave, Mary. *The Earlier French Musicians (1632-1834).* London: K. Paul, Trench, Trubner, 1917.

Harris, Simon. "Lully, Corelli, Muffat and the Eighteenth-century Orchestral String Body." *Music and Letters* 54 (1973):197-202.

Hartmann, Arnold Jr. "Battista Guarini and Il Pastor Fido." *The Musical Quarterly,* XXXIX (1953), 415-25.

Hastings, Baird. "Lully, the First Unifier of the Ballet." *American Dancer* (1941), 17, 30-31.

Hitchcock, H. Wiley. "Marc-Antoine Charpentier and the Comédie-Française." *Journal of the American Musicological Society, XXIV (1971),* 255-81.

Howard, Patricia, "Lully's *Alceste." Musical Times* 114 (January 1973):21-23.

_____. "*Alceste* (London Opera Center)." *Musical Times* 117 (February 1976):53-54.

_____. "The *Académie Royale* and the Performance of Lully's Operas." *Consort* 31 (1975):109-15.

Isherwood, Robert M. *Music in the Service of the King.* Ithaca and London: Cornell University Press, 1973.

Jarry, Paul. "Lully à la Ville-l'Evêque; le no. 30 de la rue Boissy-d'anglas." *Societé de l'histoire de Paris et de l'Ile de France,* LXI (1934), 103-107.

Lacombe, P. "Lully, professeur de violon." *Chronique musicale,* VIII (1875), 167-70.

Lacome d'Estaleux, Paul Jean Jacques. "Les Fondateurs de l'Opéra français." *Chronique Musicale,* I (1837), 34-37.

Lacroix, Paul. *Ballets et mascarades de cour, de Henri III à Louis XIV (1581-1652).* Genève: J. Gay, 1868-70.

Lajarte, Théodore de. *Bibliothèque musicale du théâtre de l'opéra.* Paris: Librairie des bibliophiles, 1878.

Lance, Evelyn B. "Moliere the Musician: a Tercentenary Review." *Music Review* 35 (1974):120-30.

La Laurencie, Lionel de. "Caractère et influence de l'art de Lully." *Revue musicale de Lyon,* VIII (1910), 169-75.

_____. "Une Convention commerciale entre Lully, Quinault et Ballard en 1680." *Revue de musicologie,* II (1920-21), 176-82.

_____. *Les Créateurs de l'opéra français.* Paris: F. Alcan, 1930.

_____. *Lully.* Paris: F. Alcan, 1911.

_____. "L'Opéra français au XVIIe siècle; la musique." *Revue musicale,* VI (January, 1925), 26-43.

_____. "Les Pastorales en musique au XVIIe siècle en France avant Lully et leur influence sur l'opéra." *International Musical Society, 4th Congress Report.* London: Novello, 1912. Pp. 139-46.

Lang, Paul Henry. "The Literary Aspects of the History of the Opera in France." Unpublished Ph.D. dissertation, Cornell University, 1935.

Lange, Ina Blenda Augusta. *Fran rokokotidens musikliv.* Stockholm: Norstedt, 1912.

Lavoix, H. *La Musique française.* Paris: Librairies-impriméries réunies, 1891.

Le Cerf de La Viéville, Jean Laurent, seigneur de Freneuse. *Comparaison de la musique italienne et de la musique française.* Bruxelles: F. Foppens, 1704-1706.

_____. "Vie de Lully." *Revue musicale,* VI (January, 1925), 107-22.

Leichtentritt, Hugo. "On the Prologue in Early Opera." *Music Teachers National Association,* XXXI (1936), 292-99.

Le Prévost d'Exmes, François. *Lully, musicien.* Paris: N. P. 1779.

Lesure, François. *L'Opéra classique francais-XVIIe et XVIIIe sièclès.* Geneva: Minkoff, 1972.

_____. *Bibliothèque Nationale, Musée de l'opéra: deux siècles d'opéra français.* Paris: Bibliothèque Nationale, 1972.

Levinson, André. "Notes sur le ballet au XVIIe siècle; les danseurs de Lully." *Revue musicale,* VI (January, 1925), 44-55.

Little, Meredith E. "Dance under Louis XIV and XV." *Early Music* 3 (1975):331-40.

Mably, Gabriel Bonnot de. *Lettres à Madame la Marquise de P. . .sur l'opéra.* Paris: Didot, 1741.

McGowan, Margaret. *L'Art du ballet de cour en France 1581-1643.* Paris: Editions du Centre National de la recherche Scientifique, 1963.

Marsan, Jules. *La Pastorale dramatique en France à la fin du XVIe et au commencement du XVIIe siècle.* Paris: Hachette, 1905.

Masson, Paul-Marie. "Lullistes et Ramistes." *L'Année musicale,* I (1911), 187-211.

_____. "Musique italienne et musique française." *Rivista musicale italiana,* XIX (1912), 519-45.

Ménestrier, Claude François. *Des Ballets anciens et modernes.* Paris: R. Guignard, 1682.

Mercer, D. S. "Musical and Choreographic Embellishment of the Sarabande." Canadian Association of University Schools of Music Journal 2 (1972):7-15.

✓ Middaugh. "The Operas of Lully and Rameau." *Journal of the National Association of Teachers of Singing* 29 (1973):41-43.

Mirimonde, A. P. de. *L'Iconographie musicale sous les rois Bourbons.* Paris: Picard, 1975.

Moberg, Carl Allen. "Lully-skolan i Uppsala universitets-bibliothek handskriftsamlinger." *Svensk tidskrift,* VII (1925), 113-35.

Montpensier, Mademoiselle de. *Mémoires.* Paris: Editions Cheruel.

Nef, Karl. "Zur Instrumentation im 17. Jahrhundert." *Jahrbuch der Musikbibliothek Peters,* XXXV (1929), 33-42.

Nerêe-Desarbres. *Deux siècles à l'Opéra* (1669-1868). Paris: Dentu, 1868.

Noack, Friedrich. "Die Musik zu der molièreschen Komödie Monsieur de Pourceaugnac von Jean Baptiste de Lully." *Festschrift fur Johannes Wolf.* Berlin: Breslauer, 1929. Pp. 139-47.

Nodot. "Le Triomphe de Lully aux Champs-Elysées." *Revue musicale,* VI (January, 1925), 89-106. First printing of Bibliothèque de l'Arsenal ms. 6.542, pp. 260 ff.

Noinville, Durey de; et Travenol. *Histoire de l'Académie royale de musique en France depuis son établissement jusqu'à présent.* Paris: Barbou, 1753.

Nuitter (Charles Louis Truinet) et Thoinan (A. E. Roquet). *Les Origines de l'opéra français.* Paris: Librairie Plon, 1886.

Obelkevich, Mary Helen Rowen. "Manifestations of Philosophy and Science in the Music of Seventeenth-century France." Ph.D. dissertation, Columbia University, 1973.

Oliver, A. Richard. *"Molière's* Contribution to the Lyric Stage." *The Musical Quarterly,* XXXIII (1947), 350-64.

Parodies du nouveau théâtre italien. . .avec le airs gravés, Les. Paris: Briasson, 1738.

Pellisson, Maurice. *Les Comédies-ballets de Molière.* Paris: Hachette, 1914.

Perrault, Charles. *Eloge de J.-B. Lully surintendant de la musique du Roi.* Unpublished.

_____. *Les Hommes illustrés qui ont paru en France pendant ce siècle.* Paris: A. Dezallier, 1696.

_____. *Mémoires.* Paris. Paris: Bonnefon, 1909.

Phipson, T. Lamb. "Episodes in the Life of Giovanni-Battista Lulli." *The Strad*, XV (1904), 124-25, 135, 179, 211, 245.

Pougin, Arthur. *Un Directeur d'opéra au dix-huitième siècle; l'opéra sous l'ancien régime; l'opera sous la révolution.* Paris: Fischbacher, 1914.

————. "Lully."   *Chronique musicale*, VI (1874), 256-60.

————. *Molière et l'opéra-comique.*   Paris: J. Bauer, 1882.

————. "L'Orchestre de Lully."   *Le Ménestrel* LXII (1896), 44-45, 59-60, 67-68, 76, 83-84, 91-92, 99-100.

————. "Les Origines de l'opéra francais: Cambert et Lully."   *Revue d'art dramatique Année 6*, XXI (1891), 129-55.

————. *Les Vrais createurs de l'opéra français, Perrin et Cambert.* Paris: Charvay, 1881.

Prod'homme, Jacques Gabriel.   "The Economic Status of Musicians in France until the French Revolution."   *The Musical Quarterly, XVI (1930), 83-100.*

————. "A Musical Map of Paris."   *The Musical Quarterly*, XVIII (1932), 608-27.

————. *L'Opéra (1669-1925).*   Paris: Delagrave, 1925.

————. "Pierre Corneille et l'opéra français."   *Zeitschrift der internationalen Musikgesellschaft*, VII (1905-1906), 416-21.

————. "Two Hundred and Fifty Years of the Opera (1669-1919)."   *The Musical Quarterly*, V (1919), 513-37.

Prunières, Henry. "L'Académie royale de musique et de danse." *Revue musicale*, VI (January, 1925), 3-25.

————. *Le Ballet de cour en France avant Benserade et Lully.* Paris: H. Laurens, 1914.

————. "The   Departure from Opera."   *Modern Music*, II (1926), 3-9.

————. "De l'interprétation des agréments du chant aux XVIIe et XVIIIe siècles." *Revue musicale*, XIII (May, 1932), 329-44.

————. "La Fontaine et Lully."   *Revue musicale*, IV (1921), 97-112.

————. "La Jeunesse de Lully (1632-62)."   *Mercure musical*, V (1909), 234-42, 329-53.

————. "Lecerf de la Viéville et l'esthetique musicale classique au XVIIe siècle." *Mercure musical*, IV (1908), 619-54.

————. "Lettres et autographes de Lully."   *Mercure musical*, VIII (1912), 19-20.

_____. *Lully.* Paris: H. Laurens, 1909.

_____. "Lully and the Académie de Musique et de Danse." *The Musical Quarterly,* XI (1925), 528-46.

_____. "Lully, fils· de meunier." *Mercure musicale,* VIII (1912), 57-61.

_____. "Notes musicologiques sur un autographe musicale de Lully." *Revue musicale,* X (1928), 47-51.

_____. "Notes sur les origines de l'ouverture française." *Sammelbände der internationalen Musikgesellschaft,* XII (1910-1911), 565-85.

_____. *L'Opéra italien en France avant Lulli.* Paris: Champion, 1913.

_____. "Les Petits violons de Lully." *L'Echo musical,* April, 1920.

_____. "Les Premières Ballets de Lully." *Revue musicale,* XII (June, 1931), 1-17.

_____. "Recherches sur les années de jeunesse de J. B. Lully." *Rivista musicale italiana,* XVII (1910), 646-54.

_____. "La Vie Scandaleuse de Jean-Baptiste Lully." *Mercure de France,* CXV (1916), 75-88.

Pure, Michel de. *Idée es spectacles anciens et nouveaux.* Paris: M. Brunet, 1668.

Quittard, Henri. "Le Théorbe comme instrument d'accompagnement." *Bulletin français de la Société internationale de musique* (1910), 221-37, 362-84.

Radet, Edmond. *Lully, homme d'affaires, propriétaire et musicien.* Paris: L. Allison, 1891.

Raguenet, François. *Défense du parallèle des Italiens et des François en ce qui regarde la musique et les opéras.* Paris: C. Barben, 1705.

_____. *Parallèle des Italiens et des François en ce qui regarde la musique et les opéras.* Paris: J. Moreau, 1602 i.e., 1702.

Riccoboni, Luigi. *Réflexions historiques et critiques sur les differens théâtres de l'Europe.* Paris: J. Guerin, 1738.

Rigotti, D. "Molière l'opera." *Rassegna Musicale Curci* 26 (1973): 25-28.

Ritscher, Hugo. "Die musikalische Deklamation in Lully's Opernrezitativen." Unpublished Ph.D. dissertation, University of Berlin, 1925.

Rolland, Romain. *Musiciens d'autefois.* Paris: Hachette, 1912.

_____. *Les Origines du théâtre lyrique moderne; histoire de l'opéra en Europe avant Lully et Scarlatti.* Paris: E. Thorin, 1895. New Edition. Paris: E.. de Boccard, 1931.

Sainte-Beuve, M. E. de. "Le Tombeau de Lully." *Gazette des beaux-arts*, V (1926), 198-208.

Saint-Evremond, Charles De Marguetel de St. Denis, Seigneur de. *Oeuvres meslées.* 3 Vols. 2d ed. Londres: Tonson, 1709.

Schure, Edouard. *Le Drame musicale.* Paris: Didier, 1886.

Scott. Robert Henry Forster. *Jean-Baptiste Lully: the Founder of French Opera.* London: Peter Owen, 1973.

Seares, Margaret. "Aspects of Performance Practice in the Recitatives of Jean-Baptiste Lully." Studies in Music 8 (1974):8-16.

Sénecé, Antoine Bauderon de. *Lettre de Clement Marot à M. de-touchant ce qui s'est passé à l'arrivée de Jean-Baptiste Lully aux Champs-Elysées.* Cologne: Pierre Marteau, 1688.

Sheppard, Leslie. "The French Contribution." *The Strad* 87 (November 1976):571.

_____. "A Powerful Man of Music." *The Strad* 83 (December 1972): 387ff.

Silin, Charles I. *Benserade and His Ballets de Cour.* Baltimore: Johns Hopkins Press, 1940.

Statisticus. "Notes sur l'histoire de l'Opéra." *Revue d'histoire et de critique musicales*, III (1903), 277-79.

Stenhouse, May. "The Character of the Opera Libretto According to Quinault." Unpublished Ph.D. dissertation, Columbia University, 1920.

Storz, Walter. *Der Aufbau der Tänze in den Opern und Balletts Lully's vom musikalischen Standpunkte aus betrachtet.* Göttingen: Dieterischen Universitäts-Buchdruckerei, 1928.

Stoullig, E. *Les Annales du théâtres et de la musique.* Paris: Ollendorf, 1899.

Ternant, Andrew de. "French Opera Libretti." *Music and Letters*, XI (1930), 172-76.

Tessier, André. "Berain, créateur du pays d'opéra." *Revue musicale*, VI (January, 1925), 56-73.

_____. "Un Document sur les répétitions du 'Triomphe de l'amour' à Saint-Germain-en-Laye, 1681." *Congrès d'histoire de l'art, Actes*, III (1921), 874-94.

Thuiller, William. "Lully's *Alceste.*" *Music and Musicians* 24 (March 1976):51-52.

Tiersot, Julien. "Lettres de musiciens écrites en français du XVe au XXe siècle." *Rivista musicale italiana*, XVII (1910); XXI (1914); XXIII (1916); XXIX (1922); XXX (1923); XXXIII (1926); XXXIV (1927); XXXVI (1929); XXVIII (1931), *passim.*

_____. *La Musique dans la comédie de Molière.* Paris: La Renaissance du livre, 1922.

_____. "La Musique des comédies de Molière à la Comédie-française." *Revue de musicologie*, VI (1922), 20-28.

Titon du Tillet, Evrard. *La Parnasse françois.* Paris: J. Coignard, 1732.

Touchard-Lafosse, G. *Chroniques secrètes et galantes de l'opéra depuis 1667 jusqu'en 1845.* Paris: Lachapelle, 1846.

Vauthier, Gabriel. "Documents: L'Académie de danse et Louis XIV." *Revue musicale*, VIII (June, 1908), 364-67.

Vie Musicale Belge. "Activités de janvier-fevrier 1973." 12 (1973):11-16.

Viollier, Robert. "En Suivant Guthbert Girdlestone." *Schweizerische Musikzeitung* 113 (1973):202-87.

Weckerlin, Jean Baptiste. *L'Ancienne chanson populaire en France.* Paris: Garnier, 1887.

Westrup, Sir Jack A. "The Nature of Recitative." *Proceedings of the British Academy*, *XLII* (1956), 27-43.

Winterfeld, Carl Von. *Alceste, 1674, 1726, 1769, 1776, von Lulli, Händel und Gluck.* Berlin: Bote & Bock, 1851.

Zanetti, Dina. "Quell'intrigante di Lulli." *La Scala*, LVI (1954), 18-20.

Historical, Theatrical, and Literary Sources

Anecdotes dramatiques; contenant toutes les pièces de théâtre. . .joués à Paris. . .jusqu'à l'année 1775. Paris: Duchesne, 1775.

Aristotle's Poetics. Translation and analysis by Kenneth A. Telford. Chicago: Henry Regnery Company, 1961.

Aristotle. *On Poetry and Music.* Translated by S. H. Butcher. Edited by Milton C. Nahm. Indianapolis, Indiana: The Bobbs-Merrill Co., Inc. 1956.

_____. *On Poetry and Style.* Translated by G. M. A. Grube. Indianapolis, Indiana: The Bobbs-Merrill Co., Inc., 1958.

Arnaldi, Conte Enea. *Idea di un teatro nelle principali sue parte simile a' teatri antichi.* Vicenza: A. Veronese, 1762.

Aubignac, François Hédelin, abbé d'. *La Pratique du théâtre.* Amsterdam: J. F. Bernard, 1715.   (Reprinted, Algers: J. Carbonel, 1927.)

_____. *The Whole Art of the Stage.* Translator unknown. London: 1684. (Reprinted, New York: Benjamin Blom, Inc., 1968.)

Baret, Eugène. *De l'Amadis de Gaule et de son influence sur les moeurs et la littérature au XVIe et au XVII siècle avec une notice bibliographique.* Paris: Librairie de Firmin-

Didot Frères, Fils & Cie., 1873.

Benichou, Paul. *Man and Ethics.* Garden City, N. Y.: Anchor Books, 1971.

Bex, Maurice. *Contribution l'histoire du salaire au théâtre en France de 1658 à la fin de l'ancien régime.* Paris: Rivière, 1913.

Boulenger, Jacques. *The Seventeenth Century in France.* New York: Capricorn Books, 1963.

Bourciez, Edouard. *Les Moeurs polies et la littérature de cour sous Henri II.* Paris: Hachette, 1886.

Bulfinch, Thomas. *The Age of Fable.* New York: The Heritage Press, 1942.

————. *The Age of Chivalry and Legends of Charlemagne.* New York: The New American Library, 1962.

Clément, Pierre. *Lettres, Instructions, et mémoires de Colbert.* Paris: Imprimerie Impériale, 1868.

Cobban, Alfred. *A History of Modern France.* Baltimore: Penguin Books, 1966.

Corneille, Pierre. *Préfaces, Discours, et Examen.* Contained in: Mantero, Robert. *Corneille critique.* Paris: Buchet/Chastel, 1964.

Delesques, H. *Pierre et Thomas Corneille librettistes.* Caen: H. Delesques, 1894.

Despois, Eugène. *Le Théâtre français sous Louis XIV.* Paris: Librairie Hachette Cie., 1886.

Desessarts, Nicolas Toussaint Lemoyne. *Les Trois théâtres de Paris, ou abrégé historique de l'établissement de la Comédie Françoise, de la Comédie Italienne & de l'opéra.* Paris: Lacombe, 1777.

Duckworth, George E., ed. *The Complete Roman Drama.* New York: Random House, 1942.

Durant, Will, and Ariel. *The Story of Civilization.* Vol. VIII: *The Age of Louis XIV.* New York: Simon and Schuster, Inc., 1963.

Erlanger, Philippe. *The Age of Courts and Kings.* Garden City, N. Y.: Anchor Books, 1970.

Euripides. *Alkestis.* Translated by Gilbert Murray. London: George Allen & Unwin Ltd., 1961.

Fletcher, Jefferson Butler. *Literature of the Italian Renaissance.* New York: The Macmillan Company, 1934.

Ford, Franklin L. *Robe and Sword.* New York, Harper and Row, 1965.

Graves, Robert. *The Greek Myths.* Baltimore: Penguin Books. 1961.

Hamilton, Edith. *Mythology.* New York.   The New American Library, 1955.

Herberay, Nicolas de, Seigneur des Essarts. *Le Premier livre d'Amadis de Gaule.* Reprint of the original edition.   Paris: Librairie Hachette et Cie., 1918.

Histoire de Paris et des Parisiens. General editor, Robert Laffont.   Paris: Pont Royal (del Duca-Laffont), 1958.

Horace. *The Complete Works of Horace.* Introduction by John Marshall.   Translated by various Hands.   New York: E. P. Dutton & Co., 1923.

Horne, P. R. *The Tragedies of Giambattista Cinthio Giraldi.*   London: Oxford University Press, 1962.

Kennard, Joseph Spencer. *The Italian Theatre from Its Beginning to the Close of the Seventeenth Century.*   Vol. 1.   New York: William Edwin Rudge, 1932.

Lancaster, Henry Carrington. *A History of French Dramatic Literature in the Seventeenth Century.*   Baltimore: The Johns Hopkins Press, 1936.

Leclercq, Louis. *Les Décors, les costumes et la mise en scène au XVIIe siècle, 1615-1680.* Paris: Liepmannssohn & Dufour, 1869.

Lewis, Warren Hamilton. *The Splendid Century.* Garden City, N. Y.:   Anchor Books, 1957.

Loret, Jean. *La muze historique ou recueil des lettres en vers contenant des nouvelles du temps écrites à son altesse Mademoizelle de Longueville dupuis Duchesse de Nemours (1650-1665).* Edited by M. M. J. Ravenel and Ed. V. de la Pelouse.   Paris: Jannet, 1857.

Lote, Georges. "La Déclamation du vers français à la fin du XVIIe siècle." *Revue du phonetique,* II (1912), 313-63.

Mémoires de Louis XIV, écrits, par lui-même, composés pour le grand dauphin, son fils, et adressés à ce prince. Edited by J. L. M. de Gain-Montagnac.   Paris: Garnery, 1806.

Molière, Jean-Baptiste Poquelin. *Oeuvres.* Edited by Eugène Despois and Paul Mesnard. Vol. VIII.   Paris: Hachette, 1883.

O'Connor, John J. *Amadis de Gaule and Its Influence on Elizabethan Literature.* New Brunswick, N.J.:   Rutgers University Press, 1970.

Pallotino, Massimo. *The Etruscans.* Translated by J. Cremona.   Middlesex: Penguin Books, 1956.

Parfaict, François. *Dictionnaire des théâtres de Paris.* Paris: Lambert, 1756.

_____. *Histoire de l'ancien théâtre italien depuis son origine en France, jusqu'à sa suppression en l'année 1697.* Paris: Lambert, 1753.

Racine, Jean. *Principes de la Tragédie, en marge de la poétique d'Aristote.* Texte établie et commenté par Eugène Vinaver. Paris: Librairie Nizet, 1951.

_____. *Théâtre complet.* Paris: Le Livre de Poche, 1963.

Riccoboni, Luigi. *Réflexions historiques et critiques sur les differens théâtres de l'Europe.* Paris: J. Guerin, 1738.

Toqueville, Alexis de. *The Old Regime and the French Revolution.* Translated by Stuart Gilbert. Garden City, N.Y.: Anchor Books, 1955.

Vieira, Alfonso Lopes. *O Romance do Amadis, reconstituçao do Amadis de Gaule dos Lobeiras.* Lisboa; Sociedad editora Portugal-Brasil, 1926.

Willey, Basil. *The Seventeenth Century Background.* Garden City, N.Y.: Anchor Books, 1953.

Williams, Grace A. "The Amadis Question." *Revue hispanique,* XXI (1909), 52-58.

Wright, C. H. C. *A History of French Literature.* New York: Haskell House Publishers, Ltd., 1969.

Zucker, Paul. *Die Theaterdekoration des Barock.* Berlin: R. Kammerer, 1925.

INDEX